M000305216

# CANNABIS
## CONFECTIONERY ART
*Krystina VanCleef*

# Cannabis

## CONFECTIONERY ART

*Krystina VanCleef*

www.mascotbooks.com

*Cannabis Confectionery Art*

The views and opinions expressed in this book are solely those of the author. These views and opinions do not necessarily represent those of the publisher or staff. This book is not intended as a substitute for the medical advice of physicians. The reader should regularly consult a physician in matters relating to his/her health and particularly with respect to any symptoms that may require diagnosis or medical attention..

**For more information, please contact:**
Mascot Books
620 Herndon Parkway #320
Herndon, VA 20170
info@mascotbooks.com

Book design by Ricky Frame


CPSIA Code: PRTWP1218A
ISBN-13: 978-1-64307-084-1


Printed in Malaysia

*Dedicated to the loves of my life, Pheonix and Grae*
*Everything I set out to do in life, I do for you.*

# Contents

# Foreword

It was the summer of 2013 and I had become manager of a medical marijuana dispensary location in Denver, CO that was shared with an infused products kitchen and extraction facility. I was the first female, minority dispensary manager for that company when I started with them, at a time when they had only one store and one cultivation facility. I went on to open store number two and three and it was at store three where Tina and I met in 2014, while working for the same large cannabis company. The store had just been converted to a combination medical and retail marijuana dispensary and the infused products kitchen was churning out products as quickly as humanly possible. The previous chef had developed a few recipes that got the company selling on January 1, 2014, but that was nothing compared to the magic that would soon happen once Tina became the infused products kitchen manager and central new product developer. She arrived with enthusiasm and a passion for confectionary art. Her background in food science and pastry prepared her well to create decadent infused truffles, perfectly chewy gummies, and sensational baked goods, all with just the right amount of cannabis permitted by the newly minted adult-use regulations.

Our relationship deepened in the following months as I left dispensary management and moved to the corporate office as the company's first technical writer. After all, I had a degree in English with a writing emphasis and expertise in managing dispensaries, so I was a good fit to continue growing the company through the creation of compliant documentation. To meet a looming regulatory deadline on March 1, 2014 requiring all manufactures to have standard operating procedures for every flavor and variety of edible they produced, I worked directly with Tina to capture her every recipe and production step in detailed documents. I am proud to say that thanks to our shared efforts, that company was the first to be acknowledged by the Colorado Department of Revenue, Marijuana Enforcement Division as being actively compliant with the new regulations by the deadline!

Since I had grown up cooking and baking with both my mother and grandmother and spent many years in college working in food service and commercial kitchens, I felt very comfortable in Tina's happy place, her kitchen. She welcomed me like a friend and shared all her tips, tricks, and secrets. That is exactly what is about to happen to you. Reading this book feels like you are sitting on a stool at the kitchen island in your friend Tina's house, learning about and receiving hands-on instruction from a consummate professional, all while laughing and having the time of

your life! If you have just the tiniest bit of comfort or familiarity in the kitchen, you can tackle any of the recipes in this book. Tina demystifies the art of infusion in chapter two, before embarking on a dive into the exciting world of terpenes. While terpenes may be a new concept to a budding edible chef (pun intended), for cannabis industry experts like myself, it is thrilling to see information about terpenes being published for a large consumer audience. Every person will build on their existing cannabis and cooking knowledge after reading this book, no question. The book is also designed so that you can skip from one recipe to another with ease, once you have mastered the basics of infusion. Filled with enticing photos of the mouth-watering treats, you will get the munchies or experience a powerful desire for a sweet while reading.

I could not help but recall when I first tried one of Tina's recipes, a key lime truffle, and I fell in love. The white chocolate truffle shell broke in my mouth and the citrus-enhanced center melted so smoothly on my tongue. Her techniques for making perfect truffles like those are in the *Truffles and Chocolate* chapter. I am sure you will fall as equally deep in love with her truffles, as I did. Throughout the book, the pro tips and suggestions on equipment and technique are sure to improve your cannabis culinary skills and make you better in the kitchen generally. Regardless of whether you are completely new to infused cooking or are a professional edible chef seeking to try playful new flavor combinations, *Cannabis Confectionary Art* delivers tested recipes with expert-level techniques in a fun and conversational tone. Take your time and enjoy the ride as you travel through a world of sweet, sour, melty, crunchy, and smooth. Your taste buds and any friends you share with are sure to thank you. Grab your spatula, rev up your Kitchen-Aid® mixer, tie your apron, and let's go!

## LAYLE McFATRIDGE

*Independent Cannabis Industry*
*Consultant & Technical Writer*
*Denver, CO*

# Sweet Dreams

I'm always dreaming up new ideas, and most of my best ideas do come to me in my sleep. I'm always thinking creatively—how can I create something new? Take something classic and put a creative spin on it? Like my Galaxy Candy or my Neapolitan Chocolates. Hard candy has been around forever and so has chocolate, but how do you take that and create something new? Creativity can come from anywhere: a shape of something, a smell, a color. You just need to learn the basics and then use your imagination.

Growing up in a kitchen, learning how to make fresh baked breads, the patient art of pie dough. For me, that's where it all began. I grew up working in bakeries and worked for many fine dining restaurants, where I mastered the art of

the grand finale. How to make perfect French macarons, fine artisan truffles, petit fours, luxurious wedding cakes, and complex plated desserts. In baking and pastry school, they teach you that each plated dessert must have different textural elements to it. A crunch, a cold, a hot element, a sauce or cream, it must be composed like a work of art. It has to be visually stunning and make sense at the same time. You can't put peanut butter with cotton candy and coconut caramel; it just doesn't make sense. It's better to have a theme or an idea that you can build on.

Say you want to make coffee and donuts. You can certainly brew a cup of coffee and fry up some beignets; don't get me wrong, that is comfort food and nostalgic. But what if you took it a step further and made a coffee cake with caramel espresso anglaise and toffee tuile? What if you made a coffee-infused donut with cookie butter ice cream; what if you made a coffee and donut milkshake? You see where I'm going with this? Think of something classic, like banana cream pie—what can you do with that, how can you re-invent it? Try new things! Maybe it'll work out and maybe it won't, but the fun is in the experience.

It was there in fine dining that cannabis found me. I never would've imagined in my wildest dreams when I first entered my culinary career that one day I would be developing some of the best and most beautiful product lines for the biggest cannabis companies in the world. But there I was, elbows deep in frosting, when a server came in and said that a customer asked to see the chef. So, I went out and the man said, "This is the best dessert I've ever tasted. Have you ever thought about pursuing a career in cannabis?"

And I said, "I don't know, I never even thought it was on option." This was way back in late 2010 when marijuana had just become legal medically in Colorado. So, I said, "Sure, if the price is right."

And he said, "Name it," and so it began. I put my notice in and for the first time, went to work for an edible company. I worked there for a few years and was then offered a chance to work for a bigger company. I accepted the offer. Ironically, my first day on the job was the first day of legal recreational marijuana sales. You no longer had to have a medical card and ailment to shop for marijuana-infused products.

I remember the line of people: it was four-people wide and all the way around the entire city block. It was an amazing sight, and I felt happy to be a part of history, the start of the green rush. I still have a picture of it. I worked for that company for four years and developed several successful award-winning product lines using my knowledge and experience that I gained as a pastry chef and food scientist. I won numerous awards, including a 1st Place Cannabis Connoisseurs Cup and a 3rd Place High Times World Cannabis Cup for Best CBD Edible, among many others.

Still climbing the ladder in my career, I left this company and was offered a position for an even bigger company. I started as a consultant and was hired to fix some shelf stability issues with their current product line. I fixed them in five hours and was immediately offered a position. I developed several exciting and new products, including a first to market recreational CBD water and two tincture lines, one of them being the first to market recreational CBD pet tincture line. It is exciting that I was able to share the knowledge of product development I had learned before entering a profession in cannabis to create something new and exciting.

Applying cannabis to confections is where the real magic happens. But with a little help from me and a few quick lessons in basic food science, you will be whipping up edibles at home like a professional chef in no time.

Always remember to practice unending patience, that mistakes are part of the learning process, that giving up is never an option, and most of all, to have some fun with it!

# CHAPTER ONE

# Ingredients- Tools- Techniques

*Quality ingredients for candy-making success!*

As I mentioned in my introduction, most of my experience comes from working in fine dining and from my education in food science, where people are looking for the best of the best, so naturally we are taught to source the highest quality ingredients. In the cannabis confectionery world, we are given a huge advantage over other candy markets because we are adding a "special" ingredient so we can charge $20.00 for a chocolate bar, whereas you would never pay that for a Hershey bar. This gives us more room in our cost of goods to afford much higher quality ingredients.

These are my go-tos and have been since before I entered cannabis. (See resources guide.)

Making candy is an art, and to make things correctly you must follow each recipe very carefully. Candy comes in many varieties, but the two types you will most commonly see are candy and chocolate confections. Ok; let's talk about ingredients.

**SUGAR:** The main sugars used in candy are sucrose (AKA granulated white sugar) which is what I use; there are also raw sugars (brown sugar, beet sugar etc). Depending on what you are making, you will most likely only be using sucrose. Be careful trying to substitute brown sugar for sucrose, as it has molasses in it and can change the flavor and appearance profile. I also like superfine sugar because it dissolves quickly.

**SUGAR ALCOHOLS**: Sorbitol is a polyol; polyols are a humectant and reduce water activity and control crystallization. I use this in my classic gummy recipes. Malitol is also a sugar alcohol used in sugar free confections and gum. Isomalt is another type of sugar alcohol with a low glycemic index it's safer for diabetics and so most use it in sugar-free candy. I use it to repel humidity.

**GLUCOSE**: My go-to is 42 DE corn syrup. It is an acid enzyme converted syrup, and it's much sweeter and thicker (more viscous) than regular corn syrup. The lower viscosity and higher brix make it an excellent choice for candy making. I use this in place of regular corn syrup so that I can reduce the amount needed. Too much corn syrup and your candies will absorb more moisture from the air and become sticky. If you can't find this, it's okay to substitute regular corn syrup.

**MALIC ACID**: This magical ingredient helps maintain and lengthen flavors, so instead of hard candies getting all the flavor in the beginning and then converting to all sugar, malic acid helps to extend the flavor throughout the length of the candy. It also enhances flavor so that you can reduce the amount of flavor needed and keep costs lower. Be careful though, the order in which you add things matters. If you add this too early in the cooking process it can cause the sugar to invert, leading to discoloration. Add this at the end of the recipe to intensify flavors and reduce amount of flavoring needed. You can also use other acids, ascorbic or citric, to add new flavor experiences. These are found in my sour hard candy or sour gummies. Also be sure to ALWAYS add your color first before adding acid so that the sugar encapsulates the color as the acid will cause a chemical reaction and change the color.

**FATS**: The difference between fats and oils is their physical state at room temperature—fats are solid, oils are liquid. Oils and fats have many important uses in confections. They are used to deliver certain flavors (think butter in caramel) or to impact the texture of the final product. Fat in fruit chews reduces stickiness, butter adds smoothness to ganache, and heavy cream adds textural elements to chocolate. The higher the fat content, the richer and more stable the ganache will be.

**SALT**: Salt is important to candy making because it brightens and enhances flavor. I like to use Maldon Sea Salt Flakes. Who doesn't like sweet & salty? Match made in heaven.

**COLORED COCOA BUTTER**: Colored cocoa butter is just what it sounds like. It's pure cocoa butter with oil-soluble colors added. I love using them to add color to chocolate. Blend them in, splatter them, spray them on, stencil them, you name it.

**TEXTURE INGREDIENTS**: I love to add texture to everything I can: fuillitine, candy crunch, waffle cone bits, ground cookies, dried fruit, dried marshmallows, cereal, croquants, dried nuts...the list goes on.

**FOOD COLORING**: I prefer liquid airbrush and gel food colorings, depending on what I am making. As food lovers we eat with our eyes, and color is important in the appearance of candy. It contributes to the overall desirability of it. Let's chat about PH and food color. Some colors are susceptible to color change based on the PH or certain reactive metals, like iron and aluminum. I recommend using stainless steel pots and adding the color and flavor first before adding the acid so that the sugar encapsulates the color before it is exposed to acids. Another important thing to remember is there may be other interferents in your food coloring that could affect final product.

For example, when added to chocolate, water and propylene glycol will cause it to seize. Always use powdered colors or colored cocoa butter to color chocolate. Water-soluble colors are okay to use with candies and gummies.

**GELLING AGENTS**: There are several types of gelling agents: hydrocolloids, starches, pectin, gelatin. We will discuss the three that I use in this book.

**STARCH**: Starch is mainly used as a gelling agent to create structure in jelly candies. When used as a gelling agent, its temperature during cooking is important. In this book, I use modified food starch. Starch is also used to create different texture experiences when mixed with other ingredients.

**GELATIN**: Gelatin is a protein derived from animal bone marrow. Most gelatin is known by its bloom rating, which basically equates to the concentration and firmness of the gel. Different bloom rates can be used to create different textures. If you want more chewy, use a higher bloom; if you want less chewy, use a lower strength bloom.

**PECTIN**: Pectin is another thickener. However, pectin is vegetarian friendly because it is derived from plant cell walls. Pectin also naturally occurs in most fruits, some with higher amounts than others. Apples and citrus peels contain the highest amounts of pectin—20-35 percent. Pectin forms a clear gel, which is attractive to candy makers. Ever notice when making apple pie that the sauce starts to thicken? Natural pectin magic! There are many types and grades of pectin: HM pectin, low methoxyl pectin, confectioners' pectin (confectioners' pectin contains sugar, which helps disperse the pectin and keep it from clumping). Depending on the grade of pectin you choose and the amount of sugar grams per pectin grams, you may need to reduce the amount of sugar in your recipe.

**FLAVOR**: We will discuss flavor in more depth in the terpene chapter—I always use high quality extracts. I love flavor companies that have assortments of creative flavor blends, like margarita, mai tai, and heavy cream (used in my Blackberries and Cream Hard Candy). Your flavors need to be either oil-soluble or powdered for chocolate and water-soluble for candy and beverages. Liquid water-soluble flavors will cause chocolate to seize. Physical appearance is important because something must look good and sound good for us to buy it, right? But taste is equally important. Play around with assorted flavors and usage rates until you find the one you love for that application.

**CHOCOLATE AND COMPOUND COATINGS**: There are several types of couverture and brands out there. They are rated by percentage, which equates to the amount of chocolate liquor each type contains. There are also many blends and combinations, from 82 percent bittersweet to 45 percent milk to white chocolate. White chocolate is not actually chocolate at all. It is composed of cocoa butter, nonfat dry milk solids, flavor, and emulsifiers. Compound coating, or coating chocolate as I like to call it, does not fall under the standard identity requirements of "chocolate" or couverture, but it looks like chocolate and tastes like chocolate. I like to use it for making truffle shells because compound chocolate contains a nucleator, such as hardened palm oil, which has a higher melting point and solidifies faster than chocolate. It also contracts from the mold the same way tempered chocolate does and has the same gloss and snap as tempered chocolate. It's more of a convenience product; if you don't want to spend the time tempering, you don't have to.

**EMULSIFIERS**: Emulsifiers are used widely in the food and beverage and confectionery industry. They have many uses, including reducing the viscosity of chocolates. Emulsifiers are both oil-loving and water-loving. To emulsify basically means to mix an unmixable substance. You see this all the time, even though you may not notice it. Take salad dressing for instance; without an emulsifier, the oil phase would separate over time from the water phase. You use an emulsifier to mix them together and keep them stable. Same goes for hollandaise and mayonnaise.

**TITANIUM DIOXIDE**: Titanium dioxide is a natural ingredient derived from minerals. It is commonly used for its whitening properties. I like to use it as a textural element in hard candy. Milk solids can also be used in hard candy to add creaminess.

# TOOLS AND TECHNIQUES:

These are my go-to tools that are must haves for my toolbox.

**SCALE**: This piece of equipment is crucial to making edibles. Why? Candy is a delicate art that requires exact measurements to make edibles with precision and ensure that every piece is perfectly infused. A digital scale is a MUST. I prefer to use a jewelry scale that goes to the 100th decimal place for accuracy. These are very expensive, so if you can't get one you can find a great digital scale online—just be sure it goes to at least the hundredth decimal place.

**CANDY THERMOMETER**: Thermo pen is my preferred weapon of choice. They are used by health inspectors and are extremely accurate, which is important because in candy making a degree over or under in any recipe can make a stark difference in final product. Oven-safe digital thermometers are also great because you can set temperature alerts and the probes wont melt. Classic candy thermometers also work just fine, just be sure you keep an eye on them.

**PASTRY BAGS AND SUGAR GLOVES**: Working with hot sugar is like working with napalm. Just kidding, but hot sugar can be extremely dangerous, so whether you are piping hot gummy or pouring candy, it is important to have heat resistant piping bags and sugar gloves. You can find both items online, just search "sugar gloves." You never want to try to pipe hard candy, but the bags can be used to pipe gummies.

**CANDY MOLDS AND CHOCOLATE MOLDS**: It is difficult to make exact edibles without molds, and you can

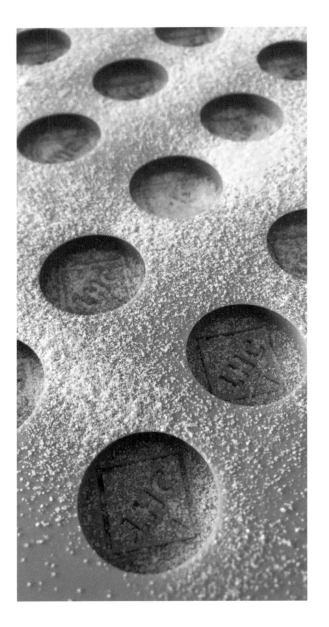

use any shape or size you would like, but make sure they are either silicone or polycarbonate. I like to use polycarbonate for chocolate; it helps to have a flat surface for scraping, and chocolates release easily and develop a nice shine. I like to use silicone for gummies and other confections because they are flexible and you can push things out easier.

**CHOCOLATE TEMPERING MACHINE**: Obviously, I don't carry this around, but it is a must for my home and work kitchens. At home I have a 2-pound tempering machine, which is relatively inexpensive. If you cannot afford a tempering machine, I would suggest substituting coating chocolate for tempered chocolate. Don't just try to melt chocolate chips, as it will take the chocolate out of temper and it won't set correctly. Coating chocolate will harden the same as tempered chocolate, and all you do is melt it. Melting temperatures are located on the side of the box; try not to exceed melting temperatures or the coating chocolate will bloom.

**AIRBRUSH AND PAINT BRUSHES**: Confection is an art, and so we use artist tools. I always say that the hardware store is a pastry chef's best friend. I use small decorating paintbrushes to put finishing touches on my truffles and bars. I also love to use the airbrush for decorating. You can find an airbrush for home-use like the one I have for around a hundred dollars. Make sure you use airbrush food coloring or colored cocoa butter. Do not use regular airbrush paint.

**BRIX METER:** A brix meter is used to measure the sucrose content of a solution. In the case of hard candies and gummies, as the water evaporates and the sugar content increases so does the percentage brix. Make sure you get a refractometer that measures up to 100 degrees brix. They are simple to use; you just use a pipette to drip a drop of solution onto the plate, close the lid, and look through the hole. The reading will show up in another color. I use this for my pectin gummies.

**MISCELLANEOUS TOOLS:** It's always good to have a good chocolate scraper, a pastry brush with larger bristles for washing down sugar crystals, a high heat rubber spatula, small offset spatulas, and a plastic bench scraper.

# PRO TIPS:

**TEMPERING CHOCOLATE:** Tempering chocolate is a very delicate and sometimes confusing art. It is probably one of the most difficult things to teach someone how to do by hand. So, unless you are very skilled I recommend using a tempering machine. All you do is push a few buttons and add and remove chocolate seed. If you don't feel up to this task at home, just use compound chocolate—there's no need to temper, just melt and pour.

**SUGAR WORK:** Working with hot sugar masses is sometimes a sticky and dangerous task. I recommend you always wear sugar gloves to protect your hands and arms, never leave a pot of sugar unattended, and be sure to use water and a pastry brush to wash down sugar crystals from the sides of the pot. This is important because sugar desperately wants to be sugar again, so any of those small sucrose crystals that come into contact with sugar syrup could potentially seed the sugar solution and cause it to seize (crystalize).

# CHAPTER TWO

# The Art of Infusion

All right, finally, the part that you've all been waiting for. This is by far the part that people believe to be the most difficult, but it really isn't! Once you know what I am about to teach you, you can apply it to almost anything.

Like any other form of baking, candy-making is an exact science. The "special" ingredient needs to be added at just the right time, otherwise it won't mix in or won't mix well enough and you will end up with inconsistencies in your product, otherwise known as homogeneity. One part of your brownie, cookie etc. could be more or less potent than another part, so the order and method in which you add the secret ingredient is crucial.

Now let's talk about this special ingredient. Cooking and baking with cannabis has been around for quite some time, mostly (up until the last few years) in the form of throwing some pot into a box of brownie mix or decarboxylating in your home oven and mixing with butter to make cannabutter. Others would make an ethanol tincture and add it to their cookies, candies etc. This method imparts a bitter hashy taste due to the full spectrum of plant matter and chlorophyll that has been extracted.

Advancements in the cannabis industry have come a long way, and so have extraction methods. There are several popular methods, including butane and $CO_2$ extraction, distillation, and winterization to remove fats and lipids. The infusion process has also evolved. Edible oil is very viscous, thicker than honey, and distillateis even more so, becoming almost as solid as glass when it's cold.

So how do we use this stuff? Let's talk about carrier oils. A carrier oil, or base oil, is used to dilute other oils' rate of dispersion, will vary based on viscosity (how light or heavy the oil is). In simpler terms without going too scientific on you, I mix my very viscous butane extracted hash oil, $CO_2$ oil, or distillate with a carrier oil to reduce viscosity droplet size and make it easier to emulsify.

My preferred carrier oils are coconut oil or MCT oil. Cannabinoids are fat-soluble, meaning they break down in fats as opposed to water. They are insoluble in water. Oil and water don't mix right, so to make them mix you need an emulsifier. When consumed with fat or combined with a carrier oil, their bioavailability is greater (bioavailability is the amount of substance that enters circulation into the body). MCTs trigger a rapid release of cannabinoids because MCTs are directly metabolized by the liver.

Saturated fats are important carriers for cannabinoids to be adsorbed by the body—coconut oil being 80 percent saturated fat gives cannabinoids the ability to be processed faster by the endocannabinoid system. If you want to know more about the endocannabinoid system, I encourage you to do some research.

As a home cook or chef, you are probably wondering, well where do I get this stuff? BHO, $CO_2$ oil, or distillate? You very well can't make this stuff at home—that is a huge no no—but if you happen to be lucky enough to live in a state where cannabis is legal, you can go to your local medical or recreational dispensary and get a syringe of either decarb oil or distillate. You can also go buy some wax or shatter, melt it down, and use it in the same way you would edible oil or distillate.

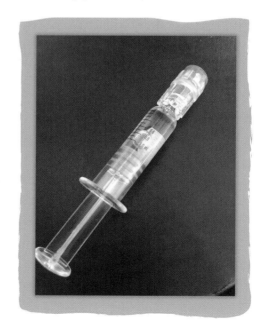

| TOTAL BATCH WEIGHT(G) | | SINGLE PORTION WEIGHT(G) | SINGLE PORTION POTENCY (MG) | HASH BATCH POTENCY (MG) |
|---|---|---|---|---|
| 3400 | | 340 | 50 | 940 |
| | | | | |
| | | | | |
| NUMBER OF PORTIONS | | 10 | | |
| TOTAL CONCENTRATE WEIGHT | | 500 | | |
| HASH OIL TO USE | | 0.5319148936 | | |

All right, now that you have it, how do you use it? How do you know how much to use?

Let's first look at how you use it. If you bought a syringe, go ahead and try to push on it. Unless the manufacturer cut the oil or distillate with another smokable or edible substance, such as PG, VG, or terpenes, you will have a challenging time getting the oil out of it. If you can, great! If you can't, then you will need to warm the oil to get it out. My preferred method is a hot water bath. If it has a cap, let the syringe soak in hot water until it is fluid enough to squeeze out. You can also wrap it in a heating pad. If you bought wax or shatter, melt it in the same manner. If the concentrate came in a glass jar, you can melt if in the oven. Once you have a melted oil, place it in a silicone bowl and add equal parts carrier oil. Then place the jar in the oven to warm it for a few minutes. Stir well with the equal parts carrier oil.

Okay, so now that you have your broken down carrier oil, how much do you use? I have included for you my formula for accurately infusing edibles. It's just simple math, and you will not believe how easy it is!

# THE FORMULA =

To get the number of portions, divide the batch weight by the portion weight—A2/C2

To get the total concentrate weight, multiply the number of portions by desired potency—C5*D2

To get the amount of oil to use, divide total concentrate weight by the potency of the oil—C6/E2

Huzzah! So easy right? You are welcome! I was told by peers and friends not to give away all my secrets, but it's just simple math; anyone can figure it out and most already have.

So, to explain in a little further detail—say you are making a batch of brownies. You'll have to make a snack batch first to get the total batch weight and unit weight to plug into your formula. No one will be upset, and you can use these later for the munchies

Make the brownies as you normally would, but make sure to weigh the batter before panning (record the weight in grams). Then bake your brownies; after they have cooled, cut the brownies into whatever size and shape you want. Next, weigh each piece to get the single unit weight (record in grams). For the oil potency, all medical and recreational dispensaries are required to test each batch of concentrate for potency residual solvents, so the potency should be somewhere on the label. When you plug that into your formula, you will convert the percentage to a whole number. So, if it's 85.90 percent, you will enter it as 859. Make sense? Now you know how much oil to use to get each piece to be exactly as potent as you want it to be. I would recommend that you start with a very low dosage—2-5mg—and then go from there. Remember that it takes up to a few hours for an edible to digest and for you to be able to feel the effects, depending on your body mass index and tolerance. So if you want to eat more, make your portions bigger but less potent so that you don't overdo it. And as with any edible you buy from the store or make at home, make sure you lock these up tight and keep them away from children and pets!

Okay, so how do I put the oil in? And when? This will vary from recipe to recipe and really depends on what it is you're making. I'll give you an example.

If you are making brownies, you would add the oil to the fat phase. In the case of brownies, the butter is the fat phase. Melt the butter as the recipe directs and then add cannabis oil; if you are adding the cannabis oil to a fat phase, you do not have to use a carrier oil—the fat becomes the carrier oil. You would warm the butter and stir very well to combine. Then just use the butter as directed in the recipe and bam! You just accurately infused brownies.

Using BHO, CO2, or distillate as opposed to cannabutter will result in a brownie, candy etc. that tastes better. The oil will also be more potent, so less oil will be needed to achieve desired potency. You will also be able to control how potent you want each piece to be instead of throwing some weed into butter and not knowing what you'll get. Sounds like an unpleasant experience to me. Also, when using cannabutter you can easily exceed the saturation point of your product and the oil will seep out.

CBD: I'm sure some of you are probably wondering about wanting to use CBD, not THC, or a combination of both. The math part may seem a little more complicated, but it's not. Let's say you want to make a batch of my gummies, and you want them to be 5mg THC and 5mg CBD per piece. First, you are going to use the formula provided to figure out how much THC you need to use with the formula above. To figure out the CBD, it works the same way. You will need to go online to buy your CBD isolate or oil. I prefer isolate.

When you buy this, it should come with a potency result; if not, check the website—most isolate suppliers advertise that their CBD is 99% pure. That's not always the case though, as I have bought isolate that they said tested at 99 and was in the 92-95 percent range. I would say go with an average of 94. So, you would plug 940 into the formula above and use it just as you would to find out the THC. Make your snack batch and weigh it, recording the number in grams. Weigh each piece to get your unit weight, plug all info into formula, and bam! You're good to go! Even though it looks like a powder, CBD isolate will not just mix in to an edible. Depending on the product, you may need to break it down from a crystalline form back to an oil using a carrier. Mix the CBD isolate with equal parts MCT or coconut oil. Warm them and stir will with a dab tool or fork.

Does Not Contain THC
KEEP OUT OF REACH OF CHILDREN
Natural
B-Caryophyllene
FOR USAGE & SAFETY VISIT
DenverTerpenes.com
KEEP OUT OF EYES
Does Not Contain THC
KEEP OUT OF REACH OF CHILDREN
11546 Colony Row, Broomfield, CO 80021
Natural
D-Limonene
FOR USAGE & SAFETY VISIT
DenverTerpenes.com
KEEP OUT OF EYES
Does Not Contain THC
KEEP OUT OF REACH OF CHILDREN
11546 Colony Row, Broomfield, CO 80021
Synthetic
B-Myrcene
FOR USAGE & SAFETY VISIT
DenverTerpenes.com
KEEP OUT OF EYES
Natural
FOR USAGE & SAFETY VISIT
DenverTerpenes.com
KEEP OUT OF EYES

# CHAPTER THREE

# Terpenes

Like marijuana, terpenes are a mixture of organic compounds produced by plants and derived by solvent extraction from botanicals or fruits and by mechanical press.

Several essential oils and terpenes are used in the flavoring of confections. Terpenes can be found in almost every fruit, plant, and herb. Pinene is what gives pine trees their pine smell and citrus fruits their citrus smell, fresh cut grass its grassy smell and marijuana strains their distinct smell. You get my point. Terpenes are also used by perfumists. So why terpenes in edibles?

All right, so everyone is familiar with (or at least starting to get familiar with) the use of terpenes for flavoring buds, distillate, and vape pens. I like to use food grade terpenes to increase flavor depth and to add effect. Terpenes also help increase bioavailability. Bioavailability is the rate at which your body absorbs things.

## TERPENES FOR EFFECT:

You may know terpenes for their therapeutic effect, like rosemary for pain or lavender and chamomile for relaxation. Cannabis and cannabidiol (CBD) are widely becoming known for their own therapeutic properties, but terpenes also have many therapeutic effects such as muscle relief, anti-inflammatories, sedative effects, aphrodisiac, calming effects, stimulating effects, and much more. I think these compounds are widely underused in edibles to enhance and add effect to cannabis.

# TERPENES FOR FLAVORING:

**LIMONENE**: Has a citrus aroma and flavor profile mostly found in citrus fruits, including grapefruit, lemons, limes, and some oranges.

Benefits: Boosts weight loss, fights bronchitis, used in treatment and prevention of cancer.

**MYRCENE**: Is earthy and fruity, most commonly found in mangoes, hops, and lemongrass.

Benefits: Boosts muscle relief and is an anti-inflammatory. Ever wonder why eating mangoes seems to increase your high? It's because cannabis also contains high amounts of myrcene.

**CARYOPHYLLENE**: My ultimate favorite! Smells hoppy and peppery. It is found in cloves and black pepper, and is also an approved food flavoring.

Benefits: Boosts anxiety relief, reduces depression, and relieves arthritis. Helps with bone stimulation.

**DELTA 3 CARENE**: Is sweet and pungent.

Benefits: Good for bone repair, arthritis relief, is an anti-inflammatory, and has been known to treat Alzheimer's.

**CREATING FLAVORS**: Brewers have been using terpenes in beer for quite some time to create flavors. Not only do terpenes enhance flavor, but they also contribute to the effects of cannabis. Be sure to only use only food grade FDA certified terpenes. Most terpenes need to be diluted prior to using. Consult with a flavorist or professional before you go dumping terpenes into your recipes. These compounds can be dangerous when used improperly or at the wrong usage rate. Add terpenes slowly and at a low usage rate; mix well if you are adding terpenes and be sure to add them to your carrier oil and cannabis oil mixtures.

**CITRUS FRUIT**

**HOPS**

**PEPPERS**

**LAVENDER**

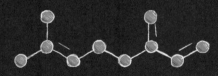

**MYRCENE**

# CHAPTER FOUR

# Gummies

Since gummies are the top selling edible in the market, it seems only fitting that we start the first section of recipes with them. In this section I will be teaching you several types, from Pate de Fruits to traditional gummies.

## PATE DE FRUITS GUMMY:

Pate de Fruits are a traditional French confection made from 100 percent pure fruit puree (you can make this yourself, just add 10 percent sucrose to fresh pureed fruit) or you can buy it. Boiron is my

puree of choice, and it is available at many local specialty food vendors. In this type of gummy, the puree is mixed sugar and corn syrup, then thickened with pectin and rolled in sugar. This type of gummy is more expensive to produce, which is why you will most commonly see it in chocolatier shops or specialty stores. But it is a great healthy vegan option.

As we discussed in the ingredients section, pectin occurs naturally in most fruits and fruit rinds. Some have higher percentages than others, so depending on the type of puree you are using, more or less pectin will be necessary. For example, apples contain a high amount of pectin, so you will use less than you would in a watermelon puree because the puree itself will already contain some naturally occurring pectin. The type and concentration of it will also vary depending on what you buy. With grocery store pectin, you will have to use a higher amount to set your gummies than if you use a commercial or confectioners' pectin. Citric acid is included in each recipe because it helps set the pectin. The amount of pectin, sugar, and acid need to be in perfect balance for the gummy to set. I like to use NH pectin—it is thermally reversible, which means you can set it, melt it, and set it again. It also sets nice and firm. The sugar citric acid mixture is important for these gummies because it helps them cure and creates a protective hard coating for the soft and chewy inside. Cure time is also important to follow in this recipe; if you don't let them cure long enough, the gummies will get soggy. Exposure to air is good for this type of gummy. You want to let them dry unwrapped so that the sugar coating on the outside gets nice and hard, protecting the chewy inside. Don't worry, sugar is a natural preservative and the sucrose content is so high in these confections that they have an extremely long shelf life, even though there is real fruit puree in them! Making this type of gummy is also a very patient process, as it involves a lot of whisking and attention.

I love flavor combinations, so most of my recipes are duo-flavor. If you prefer something simpler, just use puree and don't add flavor extract. Because this book is geared towards adults, none of these treats are meant to be shared with your kids. If you'd like, you can make these for them and just leave out the weed.

When building flavors for this type of gummy, it is important to start with a base puree and build off that. For example, if you have watermelons and you're going to make watermelon puree:

Watermelons contain a lot of water, hence the name, maybe?

Be sure to reduce the puree by boiling for a bit and letting some of the water evaporate. Then, think of what flavors pair well with watermelon. Limes, honey, pineapple, and lemongrass are just a few. Floral is also nice with watermelon. You can add more than one flavor, just be sure that they complement each other. Try not to go too far out of the box; if you add too many flavors, it can get more expensive and confusing. Have fun with it!

# BASIC FORMULA: PATE DE FRUITS

Remember that each fruit contains more or less natural pectin than another, so you may need to use less or more pectin depending on the type of puree you are using. This recipe is standard, and works will with most types of puree.

241g fruit puree
286g sugar
67g 42 DE corn syrup
15g pectin
6g citric acid
1 tablespoon coconut oil (mix with cannabis oil)

Follow instructions for measuring out cannabis oil—mix with carrier oil (coconut oil). Warm and stir well to combine. Measure out all ingredients, add everything except pectin to saucepan, and add cannabis oil. When adding cannabis oil to pan, be sure to scrape out every bit of your oil; if any residue is left behind, it can reduce the desired potency (a small offset spatula or spoon works well for this).

Bring to a boil and slowly add pectin, whisking vigorously until all is mixed in and there are no clumps. Continue slowly whisking in pectin until you have added all of the pectin. Cook and whisk constantly until thick bubbly pockets form and puree pulls away from bottom of pan when tilted.

Let cool slightly. Pour into piping bag and pipe into molds or pour into sprayed ¼ baking sheet pan. Let set at least 24 hours before unmolding. If you poured them into a pan, use a clean sharp knife to cut them into squares. Toss in sugar citric acid mix and let cure for another 24 hours.

# SOUR WASHINGTON APPLE PATE DE FRUITS GUMMY

Batch weight: 1092g | Yield: 156 (7g) gummies

This is an adaptation of the mixed drink. Science would say that things sell better when you name the fruit, such as "Georgia Peach" or "Washington Apple."

The unit weight will change based on the mold you use or how big/small you cut them, so as I mentioned in the infusion chapter, make a snack batch first to get the unit weight. Then plug into your formula. The batch weight could change to due to water evaporation, distinct types of purees, and different elevations, so I suggest weighing that too.

**Art of Infusion:**

Go buy your special ingredient and use the formula provided to figure out how much cannabis oil you need to use. Warm it and mix it with 1 tablespoon of coconut oil; melt in a microwave safe bowl for 15 seconds at the most!!! Mix very well with a fork or dab tool.

Set this aside for now and prep your sugar citric acid mix. You can increase the citric acid if you want a more sour taste or omit it if you don't want a sour taste at all. Mix 1 cup of sugar with 1 tablespoon of citric acid.

Then prep your molds—line them up on baking sheet, spray with pan spray, and dust with your sugar or sugar citric acid blend.

Using a digital scale, weigh out sugar (reserve 75g). Add to sauce pan.

Weigh out puree, add to saucepan. Weigh out corn syrup, add to saucepan. Weigh out citric acid, add to saucepan.

INGREDIENTS:
475g sugar
40g 62 DE corn syrup
6g citric acid
15g pectin
500g apple puree
4ml cranberry extract
1 ml whiskey extract (optional)
1 tablespoon coconut oil
Green food coloring
Sugar citric acid blend

TOOLS:
Digital scale
Saucepan 4-6qt
Baking sheet
Measuring spoons
Pipettes
Pastry bags
Measuring pitcher or tall glass
Rubber bands
Silicone molds
Whisk
Sugar gloves
Scissors

Weigh out pectin and remaining 75g sugar, whisk together, and set aside.

Add cannabis oil/carrier oil to your pan. When adding cannabis oil to the pan, be sure to scrape out every bit of your oil; if any residue is left behind, it can reduce the desired potency (a small offset spatula or spoon works well for this).

Bring sugar, syrup, acid puree, and cannabis oil to a boil, whisking constantly. Once the mixture comes to a boil, you can start whisking in pectin. Start by adding a small amount and whisk vigorously until all is incorporated and there are no clumps (this is similar to making gravy). Keep adding and whisking until all pectin is added.

Keep cooking and stirring until the liquid is super thick and bubbly and pulls away from the bottom of the pan when tilted. If you aren't noticing big enough bubbles or are not sure if you added enough pectin, sprinkle in a little bit more and keep cooking.

Apple thickens much faster than other purees, but you may sometimes have to sit and whisk for up to 25-30 minutes. Be sure to whisk continuously to avoid scorching.

When desired thickness is achieved, remove from heat and stir in the flavoring and coloring if desired. Allow it to cool slightly.

Put your sugar gloves on and, using a plastic measuring pitcher or tall glass, fold pastry bag inside of it. Pour gummy mixture into piping bag and tie a rubber band around the end. This will keep the hot gummy liquid from pouring out like lava and burning your hands and arms. Cut the top off of the piping bag and pipe mixture into each mold. Sprinkle with the sugar mixture and repeat with all molds. Let set to cure for at least 24 hours before unmolding.

If they don't set correctly with your desired firmness, don't flip! You can remelt them slowly over low heat, add more pectin, and repipe.

Once they've set, pop the gummies out of their molds, roll them in more of your sugar citric acid mix, line them up on sheet pan, and let them cure for at least another 24 hours.

**PRO TIP:** If you don't let these sit long enough (cure) they will get soggy. It is important to let the outsides harden; it creates an awesome texture and keeps the insides chewy. Don't worry, your patience will pay off! Another small tip: If you can't afford molds, you can also pour the gummy mixture into a 9x13 baking pan and cut them into squares.

# PEACH TEA PATE DE FRUITS GUMMY

**Art of Infusion:**

Go buy your special ingredient and use the formula provided to figure out how much oil you need to use. Warm it and mix it with 1 tablespoon of coconut oil; melt in a microwave safe bowl for 15 seconds at the most!! Mix very well with a fork or dab tool.

Set this aside for now and prep your sugar citric acid mix. You can increase the citric acid if you want a more sour taste or omit it if you don't want a sour taste at all. Mix 1 cup of sugar with 1 tablespoon of citric acid.

**PRO TIP:** If you want to step up the flavor even further, add 1-2ml of peach extract to the sugar and rub together between your fingers to blend into the sugar. You can also use a food processor to blend sugar with flavor and color.

Then prep your molds—line them up on your baking sheet, spray with pan spray, and dust with your sugar or sugar citric acid blend.

Using a digital scale, weigh out sugar (reserve 75g). Add to sauce pan.

INGREDIENTS:
475g sugar
100g 42 DE corn syrup
7g citric acid
30g pectin
500g peach puree
4ml tea extract
1 tablespoon coconut oil
 Peach food coloring (optional)
*Sugar citric acid blend

TOOLS:
Digital scale
Saucepan 4-6qt
Baking sheet
Measuring spoons
Pipettes
Pastry bags
Rubber band
Silicone molds
Whisk
Sugar gloves
Scissors

Weigh out puree, add to saucepan. Weigh out glucose syrup, add to saucepan. Weigh out citric acid, add to saucepan.

Weigh out pectin and remaining 75g sugar, whisk together, and set aside.

Add cannabis oil/carrier oil to your pan. When adding cannabis oil to the pan, be sure to scrape out every bit of your oil; if any residue is left behind, it can reduce the desired potency (a small offset spatula or spoon works well for this).

Bring sugar, syrup, acid, puree, and cannabis oil to a boil, whisking constantly. Once the mixture comes to a boil, you can start whisking in pectin. Start by adding a small amount and whisk vigorously until all is incorporated and there are no clumps (this is similar to making gravy). Keep adding and whisking until all pectin is added.

Keep cooking and stirring until the liquid is super thick and bubbly and pulls away from the bottom of pan when tilted. If you aren't noticing big enough bubbles or are not sure if you added enough pectin, sprinkle in a little bit more and keep cooking.

Peach also contains higher amounts of pectin, but you may sometimes have to sit and whisk for up to 25-30 minutes. Be sure to whisk continuously to avoid scorching.

When desired thickness is achieved, remove from heat and stir in the flavoring and coloring if desired. Allow it to cool slightly.

Put your sugar gloves on and, using a plastic measuring pitcher or tall glass, fold pastry bag inside of it. Pour gummy mixture into piping bag and tie a rubber band around the end. This will keep the hot gummy liquid from pouring out like lava and burning your hands and arms. Cut the top off of the piping bag and pipe mixture into each mold. Sprinkle with the sugar mixture and repeat with all molds. Let set to cure for at least 24 hours before unmolding.

If they don't set correctly with your desired firmness, don't flip! You can re-melt them slowly over low heat, add more pectin, and re-pipe.

Once they've set, pop the gummies out of their molds and roll in more sugar citric acid mix, line them up on sheet pan, and let them cure for at least another 24 hours.

**PRO TIP**: If you don't let these sit long enough (cure) they will turn to mush. It is important to let the outsides harden; it creates an awesome texture and keeps the insides chewy. Don't worry, your patience will pay off! Another small tip: If you can't afford molds, you can also pour the gummy mixture into a 9x13 baking pan and cut them into squares.

# STRAWBERRY MARGARITA PATE DE FRUITS GUMMY

**Art of Infusion:**

Go buy your special ingredient and use the formula provided to figure out how much oil you need to use. Warm it and mix it with 1 tablespoon of coconut oil; melt in a microwave safe bowl for 15 seconds at the most!!! Mix very well with a fork or dab tool.

Set this aside for now and prep your sugar citric acid mix. You can increase the citric acid if you want a more sour taste or omit it if you don't want a sour taste at all. Mix 1 cup of sugar with 1 tablespoon of citric acid.

**PRO TIP:** If you want to step up the flavor even further, add 1-2ml of margarita extract or lime zest to the sugar. A little Maldon salt is also nice in this recipe. Rub together between your fingers to blend into the sugar. You can also skip the sugar altogether, just be sure to spray the molds.

Then prep your molds—line them up on baking sheet, spray with pan spray, then dust with your sugar or sugar citric acid blend.

Using a digital scale, weigh out sugar (reserve 75g). Add to sauce pan.

Weigh out puree, add to saucepan. Weigh out glucose syrup, add to saucepan. Weigh out citric acid, add to saucepan.

Weigh out pectin and remaining 75g sugar, whisk together, and set aside.

Add cannabis oil/carrier oil to the pan. When adding cannabis oil to the pan, be sure to scrape out every bit of your oil; if any residue is left behind, it can reduce the desired potency (a small offset spatula or spoon works well for this).

INGREDIENTS:
475g sugar
50g 42 DE corn syrup
6g citric acid
30g pectin
500g strawberry puree
6ml margarita extract
1 tablespoon coconut oil
Pink food coloring (optional)
Sugar citric acid blend

TOOLS:
Digital scale
Saucepan 4-6qt
Baking sheet
Measuring spoons
Pipettes
Pastry bags
Rubber bands
Silicone molds
Whisk
Sugar gloves
Scissors

Bring sugar, syrup, acid, puree, and cannabis oil to a boil, whisking constantly. Once the mixture comes to a boil, you can start whisking in pectin. Start by adding a small amount and whisk vigorously until all is incorporated and there are no clumps (this is similar to making gravy). Keep adding and whisking until all pectin is added.

Keep cooking and stirring until liquid is super thick and bubbly and pulls away from the bottom of the pan when tilted. If you aren't noticing big enough bubbles or are not sure if you added enough pectin, sprinkle in a little bit more and keep cooking.

Apple thickens much faster than other purees, but you may sometimes have to sit and whisk for up to 25-30 minutes. Be sure to whisk continuously to avoid scorching.

When desired thickness is achieved, remove from heat and stir in the flavoring and coloring if desired. Allow it to cool slightly.

Put your sugar gloves on and, using a plastic measuring pitcher or tall glass, fold pastry bag inside of it. Pour gummy mixture into piping bag and tie a rubber band around the end. This will keep the hot gummy liquid from pouring out like lava and burning your hands and arms. Cut the top off of the piping bag and pipe mixture into each mold. Sprinkle with sugar mixture and repeat with all molds. Let set to cure for at least 24 hours before unmolding.

If they don't set correctly with your desired firmness, don't flip! You can re-melt them slowly over low heat, add more pectin, and re-pipe.

Once they've set, pop the gummies out of their molds and roll them in more sugar citric acid mix, line them up on sheet pan, and let them cure for at least another 24 hours.

**PRO TIP:** If you don't let these sit long enough (cure) they will turn to mush. It is important to let the outside harden; it creates an awesome texture and keeps the inside chewy. Don't worry, your patience will pay off! Another small tip: If you can't afford molds, you can also pour the gummy mixture into a 9x13 baking pan and cut them into squares.

# RASPBERRY SORBET PATE DE FRUITS

**Art of Infusion:**

Go buy your special ingredient and use the formula provided to figure out how much oil you need to use. Warm it and mix it with 1 tablespoon of coconut oil; melt in a microwave safe bowl for 15 seconds at the most!!! Mix very well with a fork or dab tool.

Set this aside for now and prep your sugar citric acid mix. You can increase the citric acid if you want a more sour taste or omit it if you don't want a sour taste at all. Mix 1 cup of sugar with 1 tablespoon of citric acid.

**PRO TIP**: If you want to step the flavor up even further, add orange zest to the sugar. Rub together between your fingers to blend into the sugar.

Then prep your molds—line them up on baking sheet, spray with pan spray, and dust with your sugar or sugar citric acid blend.

Using a digital scale, weigh out sugar (reserve 75g). Add to sauce pan.

Weigh out puree, add to saucepan. Weigh out glucose syrup, add to saucepan. Weigh out citric acid, add to saucepan.

Weigh out pectin and remaining 75g sugar, whisk together, and set aside.

Add cannabis oil/carrier oil to your pan. When adding cannabis oil to pan, be sure to scrape out every bit of your oil; if any residue is left behind, it can reduce the desired potency (a small offset spatula or spoon works well for this).

Bring sugar, syrup, acid, puree, and cannabis oil to a boil, whisking constantly. Once the mixture comes to a boil, you can start whisking

**INGREDIENTS:**
475g sugar
100g 42 DE corn syrup
6g citric acid
25g pectin
500g raspberry puree
6ml rainbow sherbet extract
1 tablespoon coconut oil
*Sugar citric acid blend
1 orange, zested

**TOOLS:**
Digital scale
Saucepan 4-6qt
Baking sheet
Measuring spoons
Pipettes
Pastry bags
Rubber bands
Silicone molds
Whisk
Sugar gloves
Scissors

in pectin. Start by adding a small amount and whisk vigorously until all is incorporated and there are no clumps (this is similar to making gravy). Keep adding and whisking until all pectin is added. Add orange zest.

Keep cooking and stirring until liquid is super thick, bubbly pockets about the size of a quarter form, and the liquid pulls away from bottom of pan when tilted. If you aren't noticing big enough bubbles or are not sure if you added enough pectin, sprinkle in a little bit more and keep cooking.

You may sometimes have to sit and whisk for up to 25-30 minutes. Be sure to whisk continuously to avoid scorching.

When desired thickness is achieved, remove from heat and stir in the flavoring and coloring if desired. Allow it to cool slightly.

Put your sugar gloves on and, using a plastic measuring pitcher or tall glass, fold pastry bag inside of it. Pour gummy mixture into piping bag and tie a rubber band around the end. This will keep the hot gummy liquid from pouring out like lava and burning your hands and arms. Cut the top off of the piping bag and pipe mixture into each mold. Sprinkle with sugar mixture and repeat with all molds. Let set to cure for at least 24 hours before unmolding.

If they don't set correctly with your desired firmness, don't flip! You can re melt them slowly over low heat, add more pectin, and re pipe.

Once they've set, pop the gummies out of their molds and roll in more sugar citric acid mix, line them up on sheet pan, and let them cure for at least another 24 hours.

**PRO TIP:** If you don't let these sit long enough (cure), they will sweat. It is important to let the outsides harden; it creates an awesome texture and keeps the insides chewy. Don't worry, your patience will pay off! Another small tip: If you can't afford molds, you can also pour the gummy mixture into a 9x13 baking pan and cut them into squares.

# CHERRY FIZZ CBD PATE DE FRUITS GUMMY

CBD has a natural sort of cherry like flavor, so I like to pair it with cherries. The fizz in this recipe comes from a molecular ingredient called Texturas Fizzy. This ingredient can be found online, just search "Texturas Fizzy." It comes in little chunks, so be sure to grind it first. It also has a slight citrus flavor, so be sure to pair it with things that work well with citrus. If you don't want to use it or can't afford it, you can also use baking soda to create a fizz. Just add 1 teaspoon baking soda to your sugar mixture.

**Art of Infusion:**

Go buy your distillate syringe, wax or shatter, and CBD isolate. Use the formula provided to figure out how much oil you will need to use. I usually make this in a 1:1 because that is my favorite ratio. I'm also a fan of micro-dosing, perhaps because I'm a wimp when it comes to edibles—I like to make these 2.5mg THC and 2.5mg CBD per piece. That way, if you want to snack on more, you can without fear of getting too high. I also feel like this ratio is a good mix for me because it takes the edge off and boosts my creativity, but I can still function. As with any edible, START LOW AND GO SLOW. Because not everyone's body mass index is the same, an edible may affect one person differently than another.

Mix the distillate and isolate with equal parts coconut oil or MCT oil, melt in a microwave safe bowl for 15 seconds or place in warm oven to melt, and mix very well with a fork or dab tool.

INGREDIENTS:
475g sugar
100g 42 DE corn syrup
7g citric acid
20g pectin
500g cherry puree
2ml lemon-lime extract
Texturas Fizzy, ground
1 tablespoon coconut oil

TOOLS:
Digital scale
Saucepan 4-6qt
Baking sheet
Measuring spoons
Pipettes
Pastry bags
Rubber bands
Silicone molds
Whisk
Sugar gloves
Scissors

Set this aside for now and prep your sugar citric acid mix. You can increase the citric acid if you want a more sour taste omit it if you want no sour taste at all. Mix 1 cup sugar with 1 tablespoon citric acid.

**PRO TIP**: If you want to step the flavor up even further, add 1-2ml of cherry extract, lime extract, or both to the sugar. Rub together between your fingers to blend into the sugar or blend in food processor. This one is good sour. If you're feeling even more fancy, you can buy some effervescence, available from specialty food vendors like Albert Uster. This will add more tang and a fizz to this gummy. Just mix the desired amount of fizz to your sugar mixture.

Then prep your molds—line them up on baking sheet, spray with pan spray, and dust with your sugar or sugar citric blend. If you are using the fizz, don't sprinkle into the mold because it will start to bubble when moisture hits it. I will explain in the finishing section how and when to add this.

Using a digital scale, weigh out sugar (reserve 75g). Add to sauce pan.

Weigh out puree, add to saucepan. Weigh out corn syrup, add to saucepan. Weigh out citric acid, add to saucepan.

Weigh out pectin and remaining 75g sugar, whisk together, and set aside.

Add cannabis oil/carrier oil to the pan. When adding cannabis oil to the pan, be sure to scrape out every bit of your oil; if any residue is left behind, it can reduce the desired potency (a small offset spatula or spoon works well for this).

Bring sugar, syrup, acid, puree, and cannabis oil to a boil, whisking constantly. Once mixture comes to a boil, you can start whisking in pectin. Start by adding a small amount and whisk vigorously until all is incorporated and there are no clumps (this is similar to making gravy). Keep adding and whisking until all pectin is added.

Keep cooking and stirring until liquid is super thick and bubbly and pulls away from the bottom of the pan when tilted. If you aren't noticing big enough bubbles or are not sure if you added enough pectin, sprinkle in a little bit more and keep cooking.

You may sometimes have to sit and whisk for up to 25-30 minutes. Be sure to whisk continuously to avoid scorching.

When desired thickness is achieved, remove from heat and stir in the flavoring and coloring if desired. Allow it to cool slightly. Also, reduce the heat once the mixture starts to boil so that it doesn't splatter and burn you.

Put your sugar gloves on and, using a plastic measuring pitcher or tall glass, fold the pastry bag inside of it. Pour gummy mixture into piping bag and tie a rubber band around the end. This will keep the hot gummy liquid from pouring out like lava and burning your hands and arms.

Cut the top off of the piping bag and pipe mixture into each mold. Sprinkle with sugar mixture and repeat with all molds. Let set to cure for at least 24 hours before unmolding.

If they don't set correctly with your desired firmness, don't flip! You can remelt them slowly over low heat, add more pectin, and repipe.

Once they've set, pop gummies out of their molds and roll in more sugar citric acid mix or sugar and fizz mix, line up on sheet pan, and let cure for at least another 24 hours.

**PRO TIP**: If you don't let these sit long enough (cure) they will get soggy. It is important to let the outsides harden; it creates an awesome texture and keeps the insides chewy. Don't worry, your patience will pay off! Another small tip: If you can't afford molds, you can also pour the gummy mixture into a 9x13 baking pan and cut them into squares.

If you chose to make the fizzy version of this recipe, spray the molds with pan spray but do not sprinkle in sugar. After they have cured for 24 hours, lightly spray them again with pan spray and toss to coat evenly. Then roll the gummies in sugar citric acid and fizz mix or just sugar and ground fizz. Let sit to cure another 24 hours.

## STARCH GELATIN GUMMY

These are a non-sugar-coated gummies. The closest thing I can compare one to is a Lifesavers gummy. They are like a gummy bear but with a slightly different, softer texture. This comes from the addition of starch. It aids in thickening and breaks down the gelatin structure into a softer gel. The outside of this type of gummy is usually coated with carnauba wax to keep them from sticking together. I love this gummy! It's my ultimate favorite. It's so versatile and you can do many things with it. Side note: Sorbitol is prone to clumping, so be sure to mortar and pestle before adding it to your sugar base.

# TIGER ORANGE POD GUMMY

Batch weight: 362g | Unit Weight: 7g | Yield: 51

Tiger's blood is a delicious combination of strawberry, watermelon, and a hint of coconut; I've also added grape to make it more visually appealing.

I made this gummy at home as a joke one day because of the not so funny videos of children ingesting laundry soap pods. Do not let your kids eat laundry soap pods! It's not funny and it's very dangerous. Instead, challenge kids to make something safe to eat. These are just as pretty, but if you make them for your kids, leave out the weed! Also, as with every recipe in this book: KEEP ADULT VERSIONS LOCKED UP TIGHT AND OUT OF THE REACH OF CHILDREN. This was a huge hit on my social media, so I thought I'd share them with you. Modified food starch is available online.

**The Art of Infusion:**

Use the formula provided to figure out how much wax, shatter, or distillate you need to use to achieve desired potency. Go buy your special ingredient. Using your scale, weigh out how much oil you need and mix with equal parts

**INGREDIENTS:**
45g sheet gelatin (230 bloom)
125g sugar
13g sorbitol
123g 62 DE corn syrup
11g citric acid
5g modified food starch
8ml tiger's blood flavor
8 ml grape flavor
Purple food coloring
Orange food coloring
MCT oil or coconut oil (equal
    parts to cannabis oil)

**TOOLS:**
Gummy molds
Baking sheet
Pastry bag
Scissors
Saucepan
Rubber spatula
Rubber bands
Scale
Measuring bowls

MCT oil or coconut oil. Warm the mixture in the microwave or oven and stir well with dab tool or fork. Set aside.

**BLOOM GELATIN**: Fill a plastic pitcher with cold water and submerge the gelatin sheets. Let them soften while you measure out the rest of your ingredients.

**SUGAR BASE**: Measure out sugar, sorbitol, corn syrup, citric acid, and modified food starch (available online and at specialty food vendors). Add cannabis oil (when adding cannabis oil, be sure to scrape out as much of the oil as possible; any remaining residue will decrease the desired potency).

**MELT SUGAR BASE**: Melt the sugars over a medium-low heat, stirring slowly with a rubber spatula. Try not to incorporate any air—this will cause undesired bubbles in final product. Once the sugar melts, squeeze out all water from gelatin sheets. Add them to the sugar base (the residual heat will be enough to melt the gelatin).

Because modified food starch is resistant to heat, you need to heat it more to thicken it. Turn the heat back on to medium and stir until the mixture is almost boiling. Remove from heat and cool slightly.

Pour ½ of the gummy mixture into one metal mixing bowl. Pour the other half into another bowl. Add purple food coloring and grape extract to the first bowl, then add ½ of your acid. Stir well, pour the mixture into the piping bag, and tie a rubber band around the end.

**CASTING**: Spray molds, but do not dust with sugar. Pipe grape mixture into each mold, filling each mold halfway. Let the mixture set to cure for at least 15 minutes. If the other bowl of gummy mixture has thickened, no worries, just place the bowl in the oven or on a burner over low heat and stir with the spatula until mixture is rewarmed. Remove from heat. Add orange food coloring and tiger's blood flavoring, then add the other ½ citric acid. Stir well to combine, pour the mixture into the piping bag, and tie a rubber band around the end. Cut the tip off.

**PRO TIP**: Always start with cutting a very small amount off—you can always go bigger, but you can't go smaller.

Pipe the orange gummy mixture on top of the grape mixture and fill to the top. Let the gummies set to cure for at least a few hours before unmolding.

# BLUE RASPBERRY GUMMY

Batch weight: 362g | Unit Weigh: 7g | Yield: 51

### The Art of Infusion:

Use the formula provided to figure out how much wax, shatter, or distillate you need to use to achieve desired potency. Go buy your special ingredient. Using your scale, weigh out how much oil you need and mix with equal parts MCT oil or coconut oil. Warm the mixture in the microwave or oven and stir well with dab tool or fork. Set aside.

**BLOOM GELATIN**: Fill a plastic pitcher with cold water and submerge gelatin sheets. Let them soften while you measure out the rest of your ingredients.

**SUGAR BASE**: Measure out sugar, sorbitol, corn syrup, citric acid (set aside for now) and modified food starch (available online and at specialty food vendors). Add cannabis oil (when adding cannabis oil, be sure to scrape out as much of the oil as possible; any remaining residue will decrease the desired potency).

**MELT SUGAR BASE**: Melt the sugars over a medium-low heat, stirring slowly with a rubber spatula. Try not to incorporate any air—this will cause undesired bubbles in final product. Once the sugar melts, squeeze out all water from gelatin sheets. Add them to the sugar base (the residual heat will be enough to melt the gelatin).

Because modified food starch is resistant to heat, you need to heat it more to thicken it. Turn the heat back on to medium and stir until the mixture is almost boiling. Remove from heat and cool slightly.

INGREDIENTS:
35g sheet gelatin (230 bloom)
112g sugar
12g sorbitol
123g 42 DE corn syrup
11g citric acid
5g modified food starch
7ml blue raspberry flavor
Blue food coloring
MCT oil or coconut oil (equal
   parts to hash oil)

TOOLS:
Gummy molds
Baking sheet
Pastry bag
Scissors
Saucepan
Rubber spatula
Rubber bands
Measuring bowls
Pipette

Pour ½ of the gummy mixture into one metal mixing bowl. Pour the other half into another bowl. Add blue food coloring and 4ml blue raspberry extract to the first bowl using the pipette. Stir well, then add ½ of the citric acid, pour the mixture into the piping bag, and tie a rubber band around the end.

CASTING: Spray molds and dust with sugar or sugar citric blend. Fumaric acid is also nice and has a different level of sourness. Pipe the first layer of the blue raspberry mixture into each mold, filling each mold halfway. Let the mixture set to cure for at least 15 minutes. If the other bowl of gummy mixture has thickened, no worries, just place the bowl in the oven or on a burner over low heat and stir with the spatula until mixture is rewarmed. Remove from heat. Add no food coloring and 3ml more of blue raspberry flavoring and the other ½ citric acid. Stir well to combine. Pour the mixture into piping bag and tie a rubber band around the end. Cut the tip off.

PRO TIP: Always start with cutting a very small amount off—you can always go bigger, but you can't go smaller.

Pipe the clear gummy mixture on top of blue layer and fill to the top. Let the gummies set to cure for at least a few hours before unmolding. Note: This recipe can also be reversed if you prefer the clear layer on top. Both ways are visually stunning and taste amazing!

# GRAPPLE GUMMY

Batch weight: 362g | Unit Weight: 7g | Yield: 51

## The Art of Infusion:

Use the formula provided to figure out how much wax, shatter, or distillate you need to use to achieve desired potency. Go buy your special ingredient. Using your scale, weigh out how much oil you need and mix with equal parts MCT oil or coconut oil. Warm the mixture in the microwave or oven and stir well with dab tool or fork. Set aside.

**BLOOM GELATIN**: Fill a plastic pitcher with cold water and submerge gelatin sheets. Let them soften while you measure out the rest of your ingredients.

**SUGAR BASE**: Measure out sugar, sorbitol, corn syrup, citric acid (set aside for now) and modified food starch (available online and at specialty food vendors). Add cannabis oil (when adding cannabis oil, be sure to scrape out as much of the oil as possible; any remaining residue will decrease the desired potency).

**MELT SUGAR BASE**: Melt the sugars over a medium-low heat, stirring slowly with a rubber spatula. Try not to incorporate any air—this will cause undesired bubbles in final product. Once the sugar melts, squeeze out all water from gelatin sheets. Add them to the sugar base (the residual heat will be enough to melt the gelatin).

Because modified food starch is resistant to heat, you need to heat it more to thicken it.

Turn the heat back on to medium and stir until the mixture is almost boiling. Remove from heat and cool slightly.

INGREDIENTS:
40g sheet gelatin (230 bloom)
125g sugar
20g sorbitol
123g 42 DE corn syrup
6g citric acid
5g modified food starch
3.5ml grape flavor
3.5ml green apple flavor
Purple food coloring
Green food coloring
MCT oil or coconut oil (equal parts to hash oil)

TOOLS:
Gummy molds
Baking sheet
Pastry bag
Scissors
Saucepan
Rubber spatula
Rubber bands
Measuring bowls
Pipette

Pour ½ of the gummy mixture into one metal mixing bowl. Pour the other half into another bowl. Add purple food coloring and 3.5ml grape extract to the first bowl using the pipette. Stir well, then add ½ of the citric acid, pour the mixture into piping bag, and tie a rubber band around the end.

**CASTING**: Spray molds and dust with sugar if desired. If you're going for a classic gummy, don't dust with sugar—just spray with pan spray. Pipe the first layer of grape mixture into each mold, filling each mold halfway. Let the mixture set to cure for at least 15 minutes. If the other bowl of gummy has thickened, just place the bowl in the oven or on a burner over low heat. Stir with the spatula until mixture is rewarmed. Remove from heat. Add green food coloring and 3.5ml of green apple flavoring, stir well to combine, then add the other ½ acid. Pour mixture into piping bag and tie a rubber band around the end. Cut the tip off.

**PRO TIP**: Always start with cutting a very small amount off—you can always go bigger, but you can't go smaller.

Pipe the green gummy mixture on top of the grape layer and fill to the top. Let gummies set to cure for at least a few hours before unmolding. Note: This recipe also looks great with no food

coloring in the green apple layer. You can also make them double flavor but only use one color (purple or green, your choice), just be sure to always add your acid after you add coloring and flavor so that the sugar encapsulates the color and the acid won't cause a color change.

# STRAWBERRY WATERMELON SPLASH GUMMY

Batch weight: 362g  |  Unit Weight: 7g  |  Yield: 51

**The Art of Infusion:**

Use the formula provided to figure out how much wax, shatter, or distillate you need to use to achieve desired potency. Go buy your special ingredient. Using your scale, weigh out how much oil you need and mix with equal parts MCT oil or coconut oil. Warm the mixture in the microwave or oven and stir well with dab tool or fork. Set aside.

**BLOOM GELATIN:** Fill a plastic pitcher with cold water and submerge gelatin sheets. Let them soften while you measure out the rest of your ingredients.

**SUGAR BASE:** Measure out sugar, sorbitol, corn syrup, citric acid (set aside for now) and modified food starch (available online and at specialty food vendors). Add cannabis oil (when adding cannabis oil, be sure to scrape out as much of the oil as possible; any remaining residue will decrease the desired potency).

**MELT SUGAR BASE:** Melt the sugars over a medium-low heat, stirring slowly with a rubber spatula. Try not to incorporate any air—this will cause undesired bubbles in final product. Once the sugar melts, squeeze out all water from gelatin sheets. Add them to the sugar base (the residual heat will be enough to melt the gelatin).

Because modified food starch is resistant to heat, you need to heat it more to thicken it. Turn the heat back on to medium and stir until the mixture is almost boiling. Remove from heat and cool slightly.

INGREDIENTS:
40g sheet gelatin (230 bloom)
125g sugar
15g sorbitol
123g 42 DE corn syrup
11g citric acid
5g modified food starch
3.5ml strawberry flavor
3.5 ml watermelon flavor
Deep pink food coloring
MCT oil or coconut oil (equal
    parts to hash oil)

TOOLS:
Gummy molds
Baking sheet
Pastry bag
Scissors
Saucepan
Rubber spatula
Rubber bands
Measuring bowls
Pipette

Pour the gummy mixture into metal mixing bowl. Add food coloring and flavorings, stir well. Add the acid, stir again, pour into piping bag, and tie a rubber band around the end. Cut the tip off.

**CASTING**: Spray molds and pipe the gummy mixture into molds.

**PRO TIP**: Always start with cutting a very small amount off the piping bag—you can always go bigger, but you can't go smaller.

Let gummies set to cure for at least a few hours before unmolding.

## CLASSIC GUMMY

This gummy is your traditional gummy bear type gummy. Typically, they are not coated in sugar. These are much more chewy than the starch gummies.

# BLACKBERRY WATERMELON LIME GUMMY

**Batch weight: 362g | Unit Weight: 7g | Yield: 51**

### The Art of Infusion:

Use the formula provided to figure out how much wax, shatter, or distillate you need to use to achieve desired potency. Go buy your special ingredient. Using your scale, weigh out how much oil you need and mix with equal parts MCT oil or coconut oil. Warm the mixture in the microwave or oven and stir well with dab tool or fork. Set aside.

**BLOOM GELATIN**: Fill a plastic pitcher with cold water and submerge gelatin sheets. Let them soften while you measure out the rest of your ingredients.

**SUGAR BASE**: Measure out sugar, sorbitol, and corn syrup. Add cannabis oil (when adding cannabis oil, be sure to scrape out as much of the oil as possible; any remaining residue will decrease the desired potency).

**MELT SUGAR BASE**: Melt the sugars over a medium-low heat, stirring slowly with a rubber spatula. Try not to incorporate any air—this will cause undesired bubbles in final product. Once the sugar melts, squeeze out all water from gelatin sheets. Add them to the sugar base (the residual heat will be enough to melt the gelatin).

Remove from heat and cool slightly. Pour the gummy mixture into metal mixing bowl. Add food coloring and flavorings, stir well, then add the acid. If you add the acid before the coloring, it will change the desired color.

INGREDIENTS:
50g sheet gelatin (230 bloom)
125g sugar
15g sorbitol
123g 42 DE corn syrup
11g citric acid
6ml blackberry flavor
2ml watermelon flavor
2ml lime flavor
Purple food coloring
MCT oil or coconut oil (equal parts to cannabis oil)

TOOLS:
Gummy molds
Baking sheet
Pastry bag
Scissors
Saucepan
Rubber spatula
Rubber bands
Measuring bowls
Pipette

**CASTING:** Spray molds and dust with sugar if desired. Pour mixture into piping bag and tie a rubber band around the end. Cut the tip off. Pipe gummy mixture into molds.

**PRO TIP:** Always start with cutting a very small amount off—you can always go bigger, but you can't go smaller.

Let gummies set to cure for at least a few hours before unmolding.

# RASPBERRY LEMONADE GUMMY

Batch weight: 362g | Unit Weight: 7g | Yield: 51

**The Art of Infusion:**

Use the formula provided to figure out how much wax, shatter, or distillate you need to use to achieve desired potency. Go buy your special ingredient. Using your scale, weigh out how much oil you need and mix with equal parts MCT oil or coconut oil. Warm the mixture in the microwave or oven and stir well with dab tool or fork. Set aside.

**BLOOM GELATIN:** Fill a plastic pitcher with cold water and submerge gelatin sheets. Let them soften while you measure out the rest of your ingredients.

**SUGAR BASE:** Measure out sugar, sorbitol, corn syrup, and citric acid (set aside for now). Add cannabis oil (when adding cannabis oil, be sure to scrape out as much of the oil as possible; any remaining residue will decrease the desired potency).

**MELT SUGAR BASE:** Melt the sugars over a medium-low heat, stirring slowly with a rubber spatula. Try not to incorporate any air—this will cause undesired bubbles in final product. Once the sugar melts, squeeze out all water from gelatin sheets. Add them to the sugar base (the residual heat will be enough to melt the gelatin).

Remove from heat and cool slightly. Pour the gummy mixture into metal mixing bowl. Add food coloring and flavorings, stir well and add the acid. Stir well again and pour into piping bag. Tie a rubber band around the end.

INGREDIENTS:
50g sheet gelatin (230 bloom)
125g sugar
15g sorbitol
123g 42 DE corn syrup
11g citric acid
6ml red raspberry flavor
2ml lemonade flavor
Maroon food coloring
MCT oil or coconut oil (equal
    parts to cannabis oil)

TOOLS:
Gummy molds
Baking sheet
Pastry bag
Scissors
Saucepan
Rubber spatula
Rubber bands
Measuring bowls
Pipette

**CASTING**: Spray molds and dust with sugar if desired. Pour mixture into piping bag and tie a rubber band around the end. Cut the tip off. Pipe gummy mixture into molds.

**PRO TIP**: Always start with cutting a very small amount off—you can always go bigger, but you can't go smaller.

Let gummies set to cure for at least a few hours before unmolding.

# TROPICAL PUNCH MYSTERY GUMMY

Batch weight: 362g | Unit Weight: 7g | Yield: 51

I dubbed these a mystery gummy because they are white. I chose tropical punch as my flavor, but you can choose any flavor you like as long as it is clear. Titanium dioxide is what makes this gummy white. It's derived from minerals; make sure you buy food grade.

**The Art of Infusion:**

Use the formula provided to figure out how much wax, shatter, or distillate you need to use to achieve desired potency. Go buy your special ingredient. Using your scale, weigh out how much oil you need and mix with equal parts MCT oil or coconut oil. Warm the mixture in the microwave or oven and stir well with dab tool or fork. Set aside.

**BLOOM GELATIN:** Fill a plastic pitcher with cold water and submerge gelatin sheets. Let them soften while you measure out the rest of your ingredients.

**SUGAR BASE:** Measure out sugar, sorbitol, corn syrup, and citric acid (set aside for now). Add cannabis oil (when adding cannabis oil, be sure to scrape out as much of the oil as possible; any remaining residue will decrease the desired potency).

**MELT SUGAR BASE:** Melt the sugars over a medium-low heat, stirring slowly with a rubber spatula. Try not to incorporate any air—this will cause undesired bubbles in final product. Once the sugar melts, squeeze out all water from gelatin sheets. Add them to the sugar base (the residual heat will be enough to melt the gelatin).

Remove from heat and cool slightly. Pour the gummy mixture into metal mixing bowl. Add titanium dioxide and flavoring, stir well, and pour into piping bag. Tie a rubber band around the end. Cut the tip off.

**CASTING:** Spray molds and dust with sugar. Pipe gummy mixture into molds.

**PRO TIP:** Always start with cutting a very small amount off; you can always go bigger, but you can't go smaller.

Let gummies set to cure for at least a few hours before unmolding.

INGREDIENTS:
50g sheet gelatin (230 bloom)
125g sugar
15g sorbitol
123g 42 DE corn syrup
11g citric acid
8ml tropical punch flavor
⅛ teaspoon titanium dioxide
MCT oil or coconut oil (equal
    parts to cannabis oil)

TOOLS:
Gummy molds
Baking sheet
Pastry bag
Scissors
Saucepan
Rubber spatula
Rubber bands
Measuring bowls
Pipette

# STRAWBERRY PINEAPPLE SHERBET GUMMY

Batch weight: 362g | Unit Weight: 7g | Yield: 51

**The Art of Infusion:**
Use formula provided to figure out how much wax, shatter, or distillate you need to use to achieve desired potency. Go buy your special ingredient. Using your scale, weigh out how much oil you need and mix with equal parts MCT oil or coconut oil. Warm the mixture in the microwave or oven and stir well with dab tool or fork. Set aside.

**BLOOM GELATIN**: Fill a plastic pitcher with cold water and submerge gelatin sheets. Let them soften while you measure out the rest of your ingredients.

**SUGAR BASE**: Measure out sugar, sorbitol, corn syrup, and citric acid (set aside for now). Add cannabis oil (when adding cannabis oil, be sure to scrape out as much of the oil as possible; any remaining residue will decrease the desired potency).

**MELT SUGAR BASE**: Melt the sugars over a medium-low heat, stirring slowly with a rubber spatula. Try not to incorporate any air—this will cause undesired bubbles in final product. Once the sugar melts, squeeze out all water from gelatin sheets. Add them to the sugar base (the residual heat will be enough to melt the gelatin).

Remove from heat and cool slightly. Pour the gummy mixture into metal mixing bowl. Add food coloring and flavorings, stir well, and pour into piping bag. Tie a rubber band around the end. Cut the tip off.

**CASTING**: Spray molds and dust with sugar if desired. Pipe gummy mixture into molds.

**PRO TIP**: Always start with cutting a very small amount off—you can always go bigger, but you can't go smaller.

Let gummies set to cure for at least a few hours before unmolding.

INGREDIENTS:
50g sheet gelatin (230 bloom)
125g sugar
15g sorbitol
123g 42 DE corn syrup
11g citric acid
3ml pineapple flavor
3ml strawberry flavor
3ml rainbow sherbet flavor
Pink food coloring
Yellow food coloring

TOOLS:
Gummy molds
Baking sheet
Pastry bag
Scissors
Saucepan
Rubber bands
Measuring bowls
Pipette
Rubber spatula

## PECTIN BASED GUMMY

This is a vegan and gluten free gummy. The texture is hard to describe, but if you've ever had gummies from a health food store, this is the exact texture and taste. This gummy is delicious whether coated in sugar or not.

One thing you will need to successfully recreate this recipe is a brix meter that reads up to 80 degrees brix.

What is brix? What is a brix refractometer? Brix is the measurement of the sugar concentration of a solution. As the sugar mass cooks (reduces) and water evaporates, the strength of the sugar solution increases.

A brix meter is a handheld device that looks like a PH meter. It has an eyehole that you look through to read each measurement (this can be adjusted by turning based on eyesight). It also has a slanted edge with a plastic lid that looks somewhat like a microscope slide.

To measure the brix of a solution or in this case, sugar solution, you will open the plastic lid and drop a few drips of your sugar mass onto the clear slanted base. Close the plastic lid and look through the eyehole. The level of brix will read as a line in color up to the brix that it is currently.

Another important thing to know about this recipe is that it calls for white grape concentrate. This is available at home brew shops, some wine making supply stores, and online. This is not the kind you buy in a can at the grocery store—this concentrate has a much higher brix than the kind you buy at the store. In this section of recipes, we are going to get a little more creative with our dosing and try combinations of CBD and THC.

**The Art of Infusion:**

Go and buy your distillate syringe, wax shatter, or CBD isolate. Do your recipe calculation using formula provided. Using your scale, weigh out the amount needed to achieve desired potency. Add equal parts MCT oil or coconut oil. Warm in a microwave safe bowl for 15 seconds or in the oven for a few minutes. Stir well to combine with a dab tool or fork. Set aside for now.

Measure out corn syrup, sugar, and white grape concentrate. Pour into saucepan and stir in cannabis oil (be sure to scrape out as much cannabis oil as possible; any remaining residue will cause a decrease in desired potency).

Cook and stir over medium heat until mixture comes to a boil. Once mixture starts to boil, slowly mix in pectin a little at a time and whisk constantly to avoid clumping. Once all pectin is added, reduce heat and cook to 80 brix. Whisk constantly to avoid scorching. Once mixture reaches 80 degrees brix, remove from heat.

Add flavor and color if desired. Pour mixture into plastic measuring pitcher or piping bags and tie a rubber band around the end.

**CASTING:** Prep your molds—line molds up on baking sheet, spray with pan spray, and dust with sugar if desired. Sanding sugar also looks nice with this type of gummy, as it has a much larger granule and adds a little extra shine and crunch.

Pour from the pitcher or pipe into gummy molds and fill to the top. Let sit overnight to cure.

**TO FINISH:** Unmold all gummies and toss in sugar if desired.

**PRO TIP:** If sugar doesn't stick to the gummies, place all gummies in a bowl spray them with pan spray. Toss around to evenly coat, then toss in sugar. Line up evenly on sheet pan and let cure for another 24 hours.

# BLOOD ORANGE MANGO PECTIN GUMMY

**The Art of Infusion:**

Go and buy your distillate syringe, wax, or shatter. Do your recipe calculation using formula provided. Using your scale, weigh out the amount needed to achieve desired potency. For this recipe, I like to make a high THC gummy—10mg per piece. Mango pairs well with THC. I would also add myrcene to this gummy, .1 percent to total batch weight. When entering the formula, put 10 for the desired potency. The amount needed will be based on the potency of the oil or distillate you buy. If you bought a gram of shatter that is 88.6 percent, you would enter 886 into the provided formula.

Measure out your cannabis oil. Add equal parts MCT oil or coconut oil. Warm in a microwave safe bowl for 15 seconds or in the oven for a few minutes. Add myrcene. Stir well to combine with a dab tool or fork. Set aside for now.

Add grape concentrate, water, sugar, and corn syrup to saucepan.

Cook and stir over medium heat until mixture comes to a boil. Add cannabis oil (be sure to scrape out as much as possible). Stir well to combine. Once mixture starts to boil, slowly mix in pectin a little at a time and whisk constantly to avoid clumping. Add food coloring. Once all pectin is added, reduce heat and cook to 80 brix. Whisk constantly to avoid scorching. Once mixture reaches 80 brix, remove from heat. Stir in acid.

INGREDIENTS:
325g 42 DE corn syrup
515g sugar
125g white grape concentrate
200g water
75g pectin
8g malic acid
4ml blood orange flavor
4ml mango flavor
Yellow food coloring
Red food coloring
MCT oil or coconut oil (equal parts to hash oil)

TOOLS:
Scale
Measuring bowls
Whisk
Piping bags
Gummy molds
Brix meter

Add flavoring, pour mixture into plastic measuring pitcher or piping bags, and tie a rubber band around the end.

**CASTING:** Prep your molds—line molds up on baking sheet, spray with pan spray, and dust with sugar of desired. Sanding sugar also looks nice with this type of gummy, as it has a much larger granule and adds a little extra shine and crunch. You can also omit the sugar.

Pour from the pitcher or pipe into gummy molds and fill to the top. Let sit overnight to cure.

**TO FINISH:** Unmold all gummies and toss in sugar if desired.

**PRO TIP:** If the sugar doesn't stick to the gummies, place all gummies in a bowl, spray them with pan spray, and toss around to evenly coat. Then toss in sugar. Line up evenly on sheet pan.

# WHITE GRAPE CBD GUMMY

**The Art of Infusion:**

Go and buy your distillate syringe, wax, or shatter. Do your recipe calculation using formula provided. Using your scale, weigh out the amount needed to achieve desired potency. For this recipe, I like to make an all CBD gummy—10mg per piece. When entering the formula, put 10 for the desired potency. The amount needed will be based on the potency of the CBD isolate you buy. If you bought isolate with a potency result of 99 percent, you would enter 990 into the provided formula.

Measure out your CBD isolate and set aside for now.

Add sugar, water, grape concentrate, and corn syrup to saucepan.

Cook and stir over medium heat until mixture comes to a boil. Once mixture starts to boil, slowly mix in pectin a little at a time and whisk constantly to avoid clumping. Once all pectin is added, reduce heat and cook to 80 brix. Add color (titanium dioxide) and CBD isolate. Whisk constantly to avoid scorching. Once mixture reaches 80 brix, remove from heat.

Add grape flavor. Pour mixture into plastic measuring pitcher or piping bags and tie a rubber band around the end.

**CASTING:** Prep your molds—line molds up on baking sheet, spray with pan spray, and dust with sugar of desired. Sanding sugar also looks nice with this type of gummy, as it has a much larger granule and adds a little extra shine and crunch. You can also omit the sugar, or you can make a sour sugar.

Pour from the pitcher or pipe into gummy molds and fill to the top. Let sit overnight to cure.

**TO FINISH:** Unmold all gummies and toss in sugar if desired.

**PRO TIP:** If the sugar doesn't stick to the gummies, place all gummies in a bowl, spray them with pan spray, and toss around to evenly coat. Then toss in sugar.

INGREDIENTS:
325g 42 DE corn syrup
515g sugar
125g white grape concentrate
200g water
75g pectin
8g malic acid
12ml grape flavor
¼ teaspoon titanium dioxide
MCT oil or coconut oil (equal
    parts to hash oil)

TOOLS:
Scale
Measuring bowls
Whisk
Piping bags
Gummy molds
Brix meter

# FRUIT PUNCH 1:1 GUMMY

**The Art of Infusion:**

Go and buy your distillate syringe, wax or shatter, and CBD isolate. Do your recipe calculation using formula provided. Using your scale. weigh out the amount needed to achieve desired potency. For this recipe, I like to make a 1:1 THC/CBD gummy—10mg per piece. When entering the formula, put 10 for the desired potency for both the THC and CBD. The amount needed will be based on the potency of the oil or distillate and isolate you buy. If you bought a gram of shatter that is 88.6 percent, then you will enter 886 into provided formula. You will need to do the calculation twice; once for the THC and once for the CBD.

Measure out your cannabis oil and add equal parts MCT oil or coconut oil. Warm in a microwave safe bowl for 15 seconds or in the oven for a few minutes. Measure out CBD isolate, add to cannabis oil, then add equal parts MCT or coconut oil and warm slightly again. Stir well to combine with a dab tool or fork. Set aside for now.

Cook and stir over medium heat until mixture comes to a boil. Add cannabis oil and CBD to mixture. Once mixture starts to boil, slowly mix in pectin a little at a time and whisk constantly to avoid clumping. Once all pectin is added, reduce heat and cook to 80 brix. Then add color. Whisk constantly to avoid scorching. Once mixture reaches 80 brix, remove from heat.

Add fruit punch flavor and whisk to combine. Pour mixture into plastic measuring pitcher or piping bags and tie a rubber band around the end.

INGREDIENTS:
325g 42 DE corn syrup
515g sugar
125g white grape concentrate
200g water
75g pectin
8g malic acid
12ml fruit punch flavor
Red food coloring (if desired)
Pink food coloring
MCT oil or coconut oil (equal
    parts to hash oil)

TOOLS:
Scale
Measuring bowls
Whisk
Piping bags
Gummy molds
Brix meter

**CASTING**: Prep your molds—line molds up on baking sheet, spray with pan spray, and dust with sugar of desired. Sanding sugar also looks nice with this type of gummy, as it has a much larger granule and adds a little extra shine and crunch. I sometimes add a little more flavor to my sugar, and you can also add color to your sugar.

Pour from the pitcher or pipe into gummy molds and fill to the top. Let sit overnight to cure.

**TO FINISH**: Unmold all gummies and toss in sugar if desired.

**PRO TIP**: If the sugar doesn't stick to the gummies, place all gummies in a bowl, spray them with pan spray, and toss around to evenly coat. Then toss in sugar.

# WATERMELON PEACH LEMONADE VEGAN GUMMY

**The Art of Infusion:**

Go and buy your distillate syringe, wax or shatter, and CBD isolate. Do your recipe calculation using the formula provided. Using your scale, weigh out the amount needed to achieve desired potency. For this recipe, choose whichever ratio you like. The amount needed will be based on the potency of the oil or distillate and isolate you buy. If you bought a gram of shatter that is 88.6 percent, then you will enter 886 into provided formula. You will need to do the calculation twice. Once for the THC and once for the CBD; if you choose to only do THC, then you will only need to calculate once.

Measure out your cannabis oil and add equal parts MCT oil or coconut oil. Warm in microwave safe bowl for 15 seconds or in the oven for a few minutes. Measure out CBD isolate and add to cannabis oil, then add equal parts MCT or coconut oil and warm slightly again. Stir well to combine with a dab tool or fork. Set aside for now.

Cook and stir over medium heat until mixture comes to a boil. Add cannabis oil and CBD. Once mixture starts to boil, slowly mix in pectin a little at a time and whisk constantly to avoid clumping. Once all pectin is added, reduce heat and cook to 80 brix. Add coloring and whisk constantly to avoid scorching. Once mixture reaches 80 brix, remove from heat.

Add flavoring and whisk again to combine. Pour mixture into plastic measuring pitcher or piping bags and tie a rubber band around the end.

**CASTING**: Prep your molds—line molds up on baking sheet, spray with pan spray, and dust with sugar of desired. Sanding sugar also looks nice with this type of gummy, as it has a much larger granule and adds a little extra shine and crunch.

Pour from the pitcher or pipe into gummy molds and fill to the top. Let sit overnight to cure.

**TO FINISH**: Unmold all gummies and toss in sugar if desired.

**PRO TIP**: If the sugar doesn't stick to the gummies, place all gummies in a bowl, spray them with pan spray, and toss around to evenly coat. Then toss in sugar. Line up evenly on sheet pan.

INGREDIENTS:
325g 42 DE corn syrup
515g sugar
125g white grape concentrate
200g water
75g pectin
8g malic acid
4ml watermelon flavor
4ml peach flavor
4ml lemonade flavor
Pink food coloring
Yellow food coloring
MCT oil or coconut oil (equal
    parts to cannabis oil)

TOOLS:
Scale
Measuring bowls
Whisk
Piping bags
Gummy molds
Brix meter

# CHAPTER FIVE

# Chocolate

**C**hocolate could be a book in and of itself, but I had to add at least a few of my favorite chocolate recipes. Most of these recipes are easy to pull off—they just take time, a dash of patience, and a sprinkle of extra effort. Remember that if you do not have a tempering machine at home, you can buy compound chocolate or chocolate glaze; these do not require tempering. Just be careful not to overheat it, which causes fat separation, also known as bloom. Do not exceed 113 degrees Fahrenheit for all chocolate glazes: milk, white, and dark. Thermal temperature guns work well for chocolate. You can buy these for a low price at any hardware store. Compound chocolate does not taste as good as fine couverture, but it hardens with the same shine and snap as tempered chocolate. My favorite go-to chocolates are Valrhona and Fechlin, and these are both available at local specialty food suppliers or online at AUI Fine Foods. They also carry the chocolate glaze coins (compound/coating chocolate). I'm also a super fan of colored cocoa butter—keep a bunch of this handy; you will need it for my chocolate recipes. I buy my colored cocoa butter online.

# DARK & WHITE MIX CHOCOLATE BAR

**The Art of Infusion:**

Go and buy your distillate syringe, wax or shatter, and CBD isolate. Do your recipe calculation using the formula provided. Using your scale, weigh out the amount needed to achieve desired potency. For this recipe, choose whichever ratio you like. The amount needed will be based on the potency of the oil or distillate and isolate you buy. If you bought a gram of shatter that is 88.6 percent, then you will enter 886 into the provided formula. You will need to do the calculation twice. Once for the THC and once for the CBD; if you choose to only use THC then you will only need to calculate once.

Measure out your cannabis oil and add equal parts MCT oil or coconut oil. Warm in a microwave safe bowl for 15 seconds or in the oven for a few minutes. Measure out CBD isolate if desired and add to cannabis oil, then add equal parts MCT or coconut oil and warm slightly again. Stir well to combine with a dab tool or fork. Set aside for now.

For this recipe, you will need two tempering machines but for the sake of those who don't have one, let alone two, let's continue as if you were using compound chocolate.

Measure out the dark compound chocolate and add half of the cannabis oil to the dark chocolate. Be sure to scrape the bowl as clean as you can; a dab tool or spoon works well for this. Melt the dark chocolate in the microwave at 30 second intervals, stirring in between each addition

INGREDIENTS:
224g white chocolate
224g dark chocolate
MCT oil or coconut oil (equal parts to cannabis oil)
Black colored cocoa butter

TOOLS:
Tempering machine
Popsicle stick
Piping bags
Chocolate scraper
Ladle
Digital scale
Measuring bowls
Chocolate bar molds

of time. It doesn't have to be exactly half because the whole chocolate bar will end up having the same amount in it. As long as you make your bars first with no cannabis oil and get an exact unit weight and plug that into your formula, they will all turn out the same potency.

Place the colored cocoa butter into a hot water bath and shake to temper. Once it is melted and tempered, pour a few drops into the dark chocolate; this will make the chocolate black.

**TIP**: How can you tell if cocoa butter is tempered? When you place the cocoa butter in a water bath, the outside melts but the inside stays solid. As you shake the bottle, the cold center interacts with the hot melted outside and the core acts as the seed, cooling and tempering the cocoa butter. To test, swipe a bit on a piece of parchment; if it sticks, it's tempered. If it separates, keep shaking and do not place back in the hot water.

Once melted, add a few drops of black cocoa butter, stir well, and pour into piping bag. Tie a rubber band around the end. Wrap in a towel and set aside for now. Measure out the white compound chocolate, add the second half of cannabis oil mixture, and melt in microwave at 30 second intervals until melted, stirring in between each addition of time. Pour into another piping bag and

tie a rubber band around the end. Wrap in a towel and set aside. Line up chocolate bar molds on sheet pan (I like to use polycarbonate bar molds).

Cut a small tip off the dark chocolate piping bag. Pipe chocolate halfway into the chocolate bar mold. Quickly cut a small tip off the white chocolate piping bag and pipe white chocolate into the other half of the chocolate bar mold. Swirl the mixture with a stick to create a marble pattern. Tap the chocolate bar mold on table to release any air bubbles. Repeat with the rest of the molds and the rest of the chocolate. Place bars in fridge to harden for a few minutes, then tap mold over baking sheet to release chocolate bars. Store in an airtight container away from children and pets.

# STRAWBERRY ROCKY ROAD CHOCOLATE BAR

This is an adaptation of the classic Ice Cream flavor. The dried mini marshmallows are usually available at your local grocery store if you can't find them I take the ones out of the hot cocoa mix.

**The Art of Infusion:**

Go and buy your distillate syringe, wax or shatter, and CBD isolate. Do your recipe calculation using the formula provided. Using your scale, weigh out the amount needed to achieve desired potency. For this recipe, choose whichever ratio you like. The amount needed will be based on the potency of the oil or distillate and isolate you buy. If you bought a gram of shatter that is 88.6 percent, then you will enter 886 into the provided formula. You will need to do the calculation twice. Once for the THC and once for the CBD; if you choose to only use THC, then you will only need to calculate once.

Measure out your cannabis oil and add equal parts MCT oil or coconut oil. Warm in a microwave safe bowl for 15 seconds or in the oven for a few minutes. Measure out CBD isolate and add to cannabis oil, then add equal parts MCT or coconut oil and warm slightly again. Stir well to combine with a dab tool or fork. Set aside for now.

For this recipe, you will need 1 tempering machine; if you don't have one, you can use compound chocolate.

INGREDIENTS:
448g White Chocolate
MCT oil (equal parts to cannabis oil)
3 teaspoons strawberry powder
3 tablespoons crushed whole almonds
3 tablespoons dried mini marshmallow
3 tablespoons dark chocolate chunks
Pink colored cocoa butter

TOOLS:
Tempering Machine
Piping bags
Rubber band
Chocolate Scraper
Ladle
Digital Scale
Measuring bowls
Chocolate bar molds

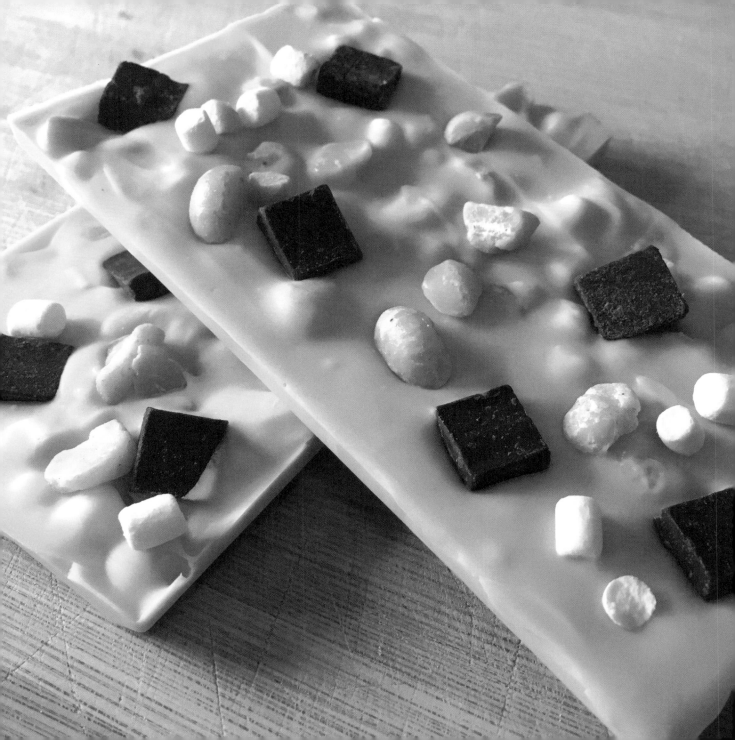

Prep the colored cocoa butter. Heat up water in microwave for 2 minutes, place cocoa butter in water bath, and let sit for a few minutes to melt the outside. Once melted, shake to temper and do not place back in the water. You will have to shake and set it down measure some things out, so make sure you go back and shake periodically until you are ready to use it. Just don't shake water into the chocolate.

Measure out the white chocolate, add white chocolate to tempering machine, and reserve 40g for seed. Add cannabis oil to the chocolate and be sure to scrape the bowl as clean as you can; a dab tool or spoon works well for this. Melt white chocolate in tempering machine according to tempering machine manual. If you are using compound chocolate just melt the 448g compound chocolate at 30 second intervals in microwave or over a double boiler. Stirring in between each addition of time. Be sure to monitor temperature so that you don't cause temperature bloom.

Once the chocolate is in temper, add your flavoring powder, and colored cocoa butter. Mix well or let spin to combine.

Line up the chocolate bar molds on a sheet pan (I like to use polycarbonate bar molds). Using a ladle, pour chocolate into the molds straight from the tempering machine. If the chocolate is too thick, you can turn up the temperature on the tempering machine a few degrees, but do not exceed 86 degrees. Once chocolate is poured into molds, use your chocolate scraper to scrape the molds clean. Tap the molds on table to release any excess air bubbles. Sprinkle the top of the bars with crushed almonds marshmallow and chocolate chunks Set in fridge to cool. Unmold the chocolate bars after a few minutes. Store in airtight container away from children and pets. TIP also you can airbrush these bars with colored cocoa butter or splatter them for more of a "wow" look.

# BLUEBERRY CHEESECAKE CHOCOLATE BAR

**The Art of Infusion:**

Go and buy your distillate syringe, wax or shatter, and CBD isolate. Do your recipe calculation using the formula provided. Using your scale, weigh out the amount needed to achieve desired potency. For this recipe, choose whichever ratio you like. The amount needed will be based on the potency of the oil or distillate and isolate you buy. If you bought a gram of shatter that is 88.6 percent, then you will enter 886 into the provided formula. You will need to do the calculation twice. Once for the THC and once for the CBD; if you choose to only use THC, then you will only need to calculate once.

Measure out your cannabis oil and add equal parts MCT oil or coconut oil. Warm in a microwave safe bowl for 15 seconds or in the oven for a few minutes. Measure out CBD isolate and add to cannabis oil, then add equal parts MCT or coconut oil and warm slightly again. Stir well to combine with a dab tool or fork. Set aside for now.

**TO MAKE GRAHAM CRACKER CRUMB:** This is just like making cheesecake crust: measure out 1 package of ground graham cracker crumbs and grind in food processor (or buy crumbs), ¼ cup sugar, 1 stick melted butter. Mix together with your hands or a wooden spoon. Sprinkle graham cracker crust onto baking sheet and bake until golden brown. (This is an important step; if you skip it, your chocolate bar will be soggy. This step also imparts a lovely caramelized flavor.)

INGREDIENTS:
448g white chocolate
MCT oil or coconut oil (equal parts to cannabis oil)
3 teaspoons blueberry flavor powder
3 teaspoons cheesecake flavor powder
6 tablespoons graham cracker crumbs
Blue colored cocoa butter
2 cups graham crackers
¼ cup sugar
¼ cup melted butter

TOOLS:
Tempering machine
Piping bags
Rubber band
Chocolate scraper
Ladle
Digital scale
Measuring bowls
Chocolate bar molds

For this recipe, you will need 1 tempering machine; if you don't have one, you can use compound chocolate.

Prep the colored cocoa butter. Heat up water in microwave for 2 minutes, place cocoa butter in water bath, and let sit for a few minutes to melt the outside. Once melted, shake to temper and do not place back in the water. You will have to shake and set it down measure some things out, so make sure you go back and shake periodically until you are ready to use it. Just don't shake water into the chocolate.

Measure out the white chocolate, add white chocolate to tempering machine, and reserve 40g for seed. Add cannabis oil to the chocolate and be sure to scrape the bowl as clean as you can; a dab tool or spoon works well for this. Melt white chocolate in tempering machine according to tempering machine manual.

Once the chocolate is in temper, add your flavoring powders, graham cracker crumb, and colored cocoa butter. Mix well or let spin to combine.

Line up the chocolate bar molds on a sheet pan (I like to use polycarbonate bar molds). Using a ladle, pour chocolate into the molds straight from the tempering machine. If the chocolate is too thick, you can turn up the temperature on the tempering machine a few degrees, but do not exceed 86 degrees. Once chocolate is poured into molds, use your chocolate scraper to scrape the molds clean. Tap the molds on table to release any excess air bubbles. Set in fridge to cool. Unmold the chocolate bars after a few minutes. Store in airtight container away from children and pets. I like to add blue colored cocoa butter to my bars, or you can airbrush them with colored cocoa butter or splatter them for more of a "wow" look.

# MUNCHIES CHOCOLATE BAR

**The Art of Infusion:**

Go and buy your distillate syringe, wax or shatter, and CBD isolate. Do your recipe calculation using the formula provided. Using your scale, weigh out the amount needed to achieve desired potency. For this recipe, choose whichever ratio you like. The amount needed will be based on the potency of the oil or distillate and isolate you buy. If you bought a gram of shatter that is 88.6 percent, then you will enter 886 into the provided formula. You will need to do the calculation twice. Once for the THC and once for the CBD; if you choose to only use THC, then you will only need to calculate once.

Measure out your cannabis oil and add equal parts MCT oil or coconut oil. Warm in a microwave safe bowl for 15 seconds or in the oven for a few minutes. Measure out CBD isolate and add to cannabis oil, then add equal parts MCT or coconut oil and warm slightly again. Stir well to combine with a dab tool or fork. Set aside for now.

Add milk chocolate to tempering machine, reserve 40g for seed, and add cannabis oil to the front of the tempering machine (be sure to scrape out as much as you possibly can, a dab tool or spoon works well for this). Follow instructions for tempering chocolate according to machine manual. While chocolate is tempering, measure out corn flakes, crushed pretzels, mini marshmallows, cookie crumbs, and toffee bits. Don't worry; all of this is factored into the batch weight and will not throw off the potency of the bar. Set aside for now.

When chocolate is in temper, add cereal, marshmallows, toffee bits, and cookie mix to the chocolate and let spin to combine. Using a ladle, pour chocolate into polycarbonate molds and, using the chocolate scraper, scrape the top clean. Repeat with the rest of the molds and chocolate. Set in fridge to cool for a few minutes before unmolding. I like to give this bar a little more texture and appearance, so I spray it with chocolate velvet spray to finish (available at AUI fine foods).

INGREDIENTS:
448g milk chocolate
MCT oil or coconut oil (equal parts to cannabis oil)
10g corn flakes
10g toffee bits
10g dried mini marshmallows
10g pretzels, ground
10g crushed potato chips

TOOLS:
Tempering machine
Chocolate scraper
Ladle
Digital scale
Measuring bowls
Chocolate bar molds

# COFFEE COOKIES & CREAM CHOCOLATE BAR

Batch Weight: 448g | Unit weight: Will vary based on mold you use | Yield: about 8 bars

**The Art of Infusion:**

Go and buy your distillate syringe, wax or shatter, and CBD isolate. Do your recipe calculation using the formula provided. Using your scale, weigh out the amount needed to achieve desired potency. For this recipe, choose whichever ratio you like. The amount needed will be based on the potency of the oil or distillate and isolate you buy. If you bought a gram of shatter that is 88.6 percent, then you will enter 886 into the provided formula. You will need to do the calculation twice. Once for the THC and once for the CBD; if you choose to only use THC, then you will only need to calculate once.

Measure out your hash oil and add equal parts MCT oil or coconut oil. Warm in a microwave safe bowl for 15 seconds or in the oven for a few minutes. Measure out CBD isolate and add to hash oil, then add equal parts MCT or coconut oil and warm slightly again. Stir well to combine with a dab tool or fork. Set aside for now.

Add white chocolate to tempering machine. Reserve 40g for seed. Temper according to machine instruction manual; if you don't have one, just melt white compound chocolate. Add cannabis oil to the front of the tempering machine (be sure to scrape out as much as you possibly can, a dab tool or spoon works well for this).

Once the white chocolate is in temper, add your ground Oreos, coffee flavor powder, and coffee grounds to the front of the machine. Then line up your chocolate bar molds. Using a ladle, pour chocolate into each mold and scrape clean with chocolate scraper. Tap the molds on table to release any air bubbles. Repeat with the rest of the molds and chocolate. Place in fridge to cool before unmolding. I don't usually decorate this bar because I find that it has a simple elegance to it, and I love the cookie specks. Store in an airtight container away from children and pets.

INGREDIENTS:
448g white chocolate
MCT oil or coconut oil (equal parts to cannabis oil)
4 tablespoon ground Oreos
2tb coffee flavor powder
2 teaspoons coffee grounds

TOOLS:
Tempering machine
Chocolate scraper
Ladle
Digital scale
Measuring bowls
Chocolate bar molds

# SALTED CARAMEL WAFFLECONE CHOCOLATE BAR

Batch Weight: 508g | Unit Weight: Will vary based on mold you use | Yield: About 8 bars

It's important for this bar that you use Carmelia chocolate. It already has a nice caramel flavor, so you don't need to add any.

**The Art of Infusion:**

Go and buy your distillate syringe, wax or shatter, and CBD isolate. Do your recipe calculation using the formula provided. Using your scale, weigh out the amount needed to achieve desired potency. For this recipe, choose whichever ratio you like. The amount needed will be based on the potency of the oil or distillate and isolate you buy. If you bought a gram of shatter that is 88.6 percent, then you will enter 886 into the provided formula. You will need to do the calculation twice. Once for the THC and once for the CBD; if you choose to only use THC, then you will only need to calculate once.

Measure out your hash oil and add equal parts MCT oil or coconut oil. Warm in a microwave safe bowl for 15 seconds or in the oven for a few minutes. Measure out CBD isolate and add to hash oil, then add equal parts MCT or coconut oil and warm slightly again. Stir well to combine with a dab tool or fork. Set aside for now.

Add milk chocolate to tempering machine. Temper according to machine instructions or melt the same amount of compound milk chocolate. Add cannabis oil to the front of tempering machine (be sure to scrape out as much oil as possible, a dab tool or spoon works well for this). Let spin to combine. Using a ladle, pour chocolate into bar molds. Scrape clean with a chocolate scraper. Sprinkle with Maldon salt and crushed waffle cone bits. Repeat with all molds and remaining chocolate. Let sit in the fridge to cool for a few minutes before unmolding. Store in airtight container away from children and pets,

INGREDIENTS:
448g Carmelia chocolate
MCT oil or coconut oil (equal parts to cannabis oil)
1 tb Maldon salt
8 tb crushed waffle cone

TOOLS:
Tempering machine
Chocolate bar molds
Chocolate scraper
Ladle
Digital scale
Measuring bowls

# CHOCOLATE BAR DUOS

Batch Weight: 508g | Unit Weight: Will vary based on mold you use | Yield: About 8 bars

These bars can be made in pretty much any variety. I chose blackberry dark chocolate and peppermint dark chocolate, but you could make any combination of white and dark or milk and white with added flavors textures.

**The Art of Infusion:**

Go and buy your distillate syringe, wax or shatter, and CBD isolate. Do your recipe calculation using the formula provided. Using your scale, weigh out the amount needed to achieve desired potency. For this recipe, choose whichever ratio you like. The amount needed will be based on the potency of the oil or distillate and isolate you buy. If you bought a gram of shatter that is 88.6 percent, then you will enter 886 into the provided formula. You will need to do the calculation twice. Once for the THC and once for the CBD; if you choose to only use THC, then you will only need to calculate once.

Measure out your cannabis oil and add equal parts MCT oil or coconut oil. Warm in a microwave safe bowl for 15 seconds or in the oven for

INGREDIENTS:
448g white chocolate
448g dark chocolate
MCT oil or coconut oil (equal parts to cannabis oil)
Blackberry flavor powder
Purple colored cocoa butter
Green colored cocoa butter
Peppermint flavor powder

TOOLS:
Tempering machine
Chocolate bar molds
Chocolate scraper
Ladle
Digital scale
Measuring bowls

a few minutes. Measure out CBD isolate and add to cannabis oil, then add equal parts MCT or coconut oil and warm slightly again. Stir well to combine with a dab tool or fork. Set aside for now.

Prep the colored cocoa butter. Heat water in microwave for 2 minutes and place the cocoa butter color in water bath. Let sit for a few minutes while you measure things out. Take cocoa butter color out of water bath and shake to temper. Periodically go back and shake until you are ready to use it. Just be sure not to shake water into chocolate.

Add white chocolate to tempering machine. Add dark chocolate to another tempering machine and temper according to machine instructions; if you don't have a tempering machine, just melt the same amount of compound white and dark chocolate. Add cannabis oil to the front of tempering machine (be sure to scrape out as much oil as possible, a dab tool or spoon works well for this). Add half to the white and half to the dark.

Once the chocolate is in temper, add your flavor powder and a few drops of colored cocoa butter to the white chocolate. I made these one at a time, so I did blackberry flavor powder and purple colored cocoa butter to the white chocolate first, then cleaned the machines and repeated the process but added mint flavor and green colored cocoa butter to the second batch.

Let spin to combine. Using a ladle, pour flavored white chocolate into piping bag and tie a rubber band around the end. Cut a small tip off the top and pipe halfway into each bar mold. Tap molds to settle chocolate. Then use ladle to pour dark chocolate into another piping bag. Tie a rubber band around the end and cut a small tip off the top. Pipe dark chocolate into the other half of each bar mold; tap to settle chocolate. Scrape clean with a chocolate scraper. Repeat with all molds and remaining chocolate. Let sit in the fridge to cool for a few minutes before unmolding. Store in airtight container away from children and pets

## TRUFFLES AND CHOCOLATE

Truffles are one of my favorite things to make! I mostly use compound chocolate to create my shells. The filling will be the infused part. Again, these take a little extra time and effort, but I'm sure you will master them in no time! Sometimes I make truffles using pre-made shells, but lately I'm in love with making my own and decorating them. So, there aren't any of that type in this book. I may just write another book on chocolate.

# SMOKED CHOCOLATE MARSHMALLOW S'MORE TRUFFLE

I love this truffle. I use smoke aroma, which can be purchased online at AUI Fine Foods. Just a tiny bit goes a long way. You can also substitute liquid smoke from the grocery store. It's my rendition of the classic campfire favorite. I'm also a huge fan of whipped ganache, so you will also need a good mixer for most of my truffle recipes.

**The Art of Infusion:**
Go and buy your distillate syringe, wax or shatter, and CBD isolate. Do your recipe calculation using the formula provided. Using your scale, weigh out the amount needed to achieve desired potency. For this recipe, choose whichever ratio you like. The amount needed will be based on the potency of the oil or distillate and isolate you buy. If you bought a gram of shatter that is 88.6 percent, then you will enter 886 into the provided formula. You will need to do the calculation twice. Once for the THC and once for the CBD; if you choose to only use THC, then you will only need to calculate once.

Measure out your hash oil and add equal parts MCT oil or coconut oil. Warm in a microwave safe bowl for 15 seconds or in the oven for a few minutes. Measure out CBD isolate and add to cannabis oil, then add equal parts MCT or coconut oil and warm slightly again. Stir well to combine with a dab tool or fork. Set aside for now.

INGREDIENTS:
448g dark compound
    chocolate
2 drops smoke aroma flavor
198g marshmallow fluff
200g milk chocolate
100g heavy cream
6TB graham cracker crumb

TOOLS:
Round chocolate molds
Chocolate scraper
Baking sheet
Piping bags
Offset spatula

**TO MAKE SHELLS**: Melt milk compound chocolate in microwave safe bowl at 30 second intervals and stir between each addition of time to avoid scorching. Once chocolate is melted, pour chocolate into square chocolate molds. I like to use silicone, but you can also use polycarbonate. Wear gloves and use your finger to swirl around and coat each cavity. Turn mold upside down and shake off excess chocolate. Scrape clean with chocolate scraper. Then turn right side up to let chocolate harden while you make the ganache.

**TO MAKE GANACHE**: Measure out marshmallow fluff and add smoke flavor and graham cracker mix to combine ingredients. Pour in your cannabis oil (rewarm if necessary). Be sure to scrape out as much of the oil as possible. Rewhip to incorporate cannabis oil and scrape down the bottom and sides of the bowl.

Using a rubber spatula, fill piping bag with marshmallow fluff mixture. Cut a hole in tip of piping bag and pipe mixture halfway into each mold cavity. Repeat with all molds and all filling.

Measure out milk chocolate and heavy cream in a microwave safe bowl and melt in microwave at 30 second intervals until chocolate is melted and cream is warm (but not too warm), 60 seconds at most. Pour chocolate and cream mixture into

bowl of mixer and using whip attachment, whip until light and fluffy. Using a spatula, fill piping bag with milk chocolate ganache and pipe into molds, filling almost to the top.

Once all mixture is piped, rewarm milk compound chocolate in microwave at 30-second intervals again and stir in between each addition of time. Pour over the top of mold and smooth evenly with an offset spatula. Scrape clean with chocolate scraper.

**TO FINISH**: Place molds in fridge to cool for 30 minutes. Turn mold upside down over parchment-lined baking sheet. Flex, push, and tap mold to release chocolates. Store in airtight container away from children and pets.

# DARK & WHITE TIRAMISU TRUFFLE

**The Art of Infusion:**

Go and buy your distillate syringe, wax or shatter, and CBD isolate. Do your recipe calculation using the formula provided. Using your scale, weigh out the amount needed to achieve desired potency. For this recipe, choose whichever ratio you like. The amount needed will be based on the potency of the oil or distillate and isolate you buy. If you bought a gram of shatter that is 88.6 percent, then you will enter 886 into the provided formula. You will need to do the calculation twice. Once for the THC and once for the CBD; if you choose to only use THC, then you will only need to calculate once.

Measure out your cannabis oil and add equal parts MCT oil or coconut oil. Warm in a microwave safe bowl for 15 seconds or in the oven for a few minutes. Measure out CBD isolate and add to cannabis oil, then add equal parts MCT or coconut oil and warm slightly again. Stir well to combine with a dab tool or fork. Set aside for now.

**TO MAKE SHELLS**: If you want to make them pretty like mine are, you'll have to melt a small

**INGREDIENTS:**
Dark compound chocolate
White compound chocolate
200g white chocolate
200g dark chocolate
200g cream (divided) heavy cream
20g mascarpone cheese
20g ground ladyfingers
½ package instant coffee

**TOOLS:**
Square truffle mold
Small paint brush
Piping bags
Chocolate scraper
Offset spatula
KitchenAid mixer

amount of white compound chocolate. Once melted, dip your artist brush into melted chocolate and swipe the inside of each mold cavity; you can also drip it, airbrush it, or splatter it—whichever you prefer. Let dry while melting dark compound chocolate.

Melt dark compound chocolate in a microwave safe bowl at 30-second intervals until melted, stirring in between each addition of time. Pour compound chocolate into round or square truffle mold and swirl around to coat the inside of each cavity. Turn mold upside down and shake off excess chocolate. Scrape clean with chocolate scraper and turn right side up on baking sheet.

**TO MAKE GANACHE:** In a microwave safe bowl, measure out the white chocolate, 100g of heavy cream, and instant coffee. Microwave for 60 seconds and stir well to combine. Pour into the mixer bowl. Rewarm cannabis oil and add to espresso ganache. Whip until it is a light and fluffy frosting consistency. Add ground ladyfingers and mascarpone cheese and whip to combine. Pour mixture into piping bag and tie a rubber band around the end. Cut tip off of piping bag and pipe halfway into molds; repeat with all molds all filling.

Next, measure out your dark chocolate and the other 100g cream. Melt in microwave for 30-45 seconds or until melted. Stir well and pour into mixer. Whip until light and fluffy frosting consistency. Pipe into the other half of the molds, filling about ¾ of the way to the top.

Remelt dark coating chocolate and pour over the top of the molds. Smooth evenly with offset spatula and scrape clean with chocolate scraper.

**TO FINISH:** Place molds in fridge to cool for at least 30 minutes. Take molds out of the fridge and flex and tap to release chocolates. Store in airtight container away from children and pets.

# BUTTER PECAN ICE CREAM TRUFFLE

**The Art of Infusion:**

Go and buy your distillate syringe, wax or shatter, and CBD isolate. Do your recipe calculation using the formula provided. Using your scale, weigh out the amount needed to achieve desired potency. For this recipe, choose whichever ratio you like. The amount needed will be based on the potency of the oil or distillate and isolate you buy. If you bought a gram of shatter that is 88.6 percent, then you will enter 886 into the provided formula. You will need to do the calculation twice. Once for the THC and once for the CBD; if you choose to only use THC, then you will only need to calculate once.

Measure out your hash oil and add equal parts MCT oil or coconut oil. Warm in a microwave safe bowl for 15 seconds or in the oven for a few minutes. Measure out CBD isolate and add to cannabis oil, then add equal parts MCT or coconut oil and warm slightly again. Stir well to combine with a dab tool or fork. Set aside for now.

**TO MAKE SHELLS**: Sprinkle ground pecans into the top of each mold cavity. You can use a triangle mold or any other shape.

Measure out white compound chocolate in a microwave safe bowl and microwave at 30-second intervals until melted, stirring in between each addition of time. Pour white compound chocolate into each mold cavity and swirl around to coat. Turn mold upside down and shake off excess chocolate. Scrape clean with chocolate scraper. Turn right side up on baking sheet and let sit to harden while you make the ganache.

INGREDIENTS:
50g ground pecans
454g white coating chocolate
400g white chocolate
6ml butter pecan extract
200g heavy cream
2ml heavy cream extract

TOOLS:
Truffle mold
Chocolate scraper
Piping bags
KitchenAid mixer
Offset spatula

**TO MAKE GANACHE:** Measure out white chocolate, heavy cream, butter pecan extract, and heavy cream extract in microwave safe bowl. Melt in 30 second increments, stirring in between each addition of time until melted. Add cannabis oil; be sure to scrape out as much of the oil as possible. Rewarm if necessary. Stir in cannabis oil and pour ganache into bowl of mixer. Using whip attachment, whip on medium speed until light and fluffy. Pour ganache into piping bag and cut the tip off the end. Pipe ganache into each mold cavity, almost to the top. Repeat with all molds and remainder of ganache.

**TO FINISH:** Remelt white compound chocolate and pour over the top of each mold. Smooth evenly with offset spatula and scrape clean with chocolate scraper. Place molds in fridge to cool for at least 30 minutes. Then flex and tap each mold to release chocolates. Store in airtight container away from children and pets.

# BANANA SPLIT ICE CREAM TRUFFLE

I'm obsessed with ice cream lately too; I'd love to someday include a chapter or book on infused ice cream. The naturally occurring fats in ice cream blend so well with cannabis. But for now, we spin-off ice cream and create something new.

**The Art of Infusion:**

Go and buy your distillate syringe, wax or shatter, and CBD isolate. Do your recipe calculation using the formula provided. Using your scale, weigh out the amount needed to achieve desired potency. For this recipe, choose whichever ratio you like. The amount needed will be based on the potency of the oil or distillate and isolate you buy. If you bought a gram of shatter that is 88.6 percent, then you will enter 886 into the provided formula. You will need to do the calculation twice. Once for the THC and once for the CBD; if you choose to only use THC, then you will only need to calculate once.

Measure out your cannabis oil and add equal parts MCT oil or coconut oil. Warm in a microwave safe bowl for 15 seconds or in the oven for a few minutes. Measure out CBD isolate and add to cannabis oil, then add equal parts MCT or coconut oil and warm slightly again. Stir well to combine with a dab tool or fork. Set aside for now.

**TO MAKE SHELLS**: First, you will need to paint the shells. Get 3 pitchers out and fill them with about 2 cups of water. Microwave for 2 minutes

INGREDIENTS:
454g white compound
    chocolate
Yellow, brown, and pink
    colored cocoa butter
400g white chocolate
150g dark chocolate
275g heavy cream (divided)
4ml banana extract
4ml strawberry extract
50g ground pecans

TOOLS:
Square truffle mold
Small paintbrush
Piping bags
Chocolate scraper
Scale
KitchenAid mixer

and place pink, yellow, and brown colored cocoa butter into each water bath. Let sit for about 10 minutes. Shake periodically to temper (be sure not to shake water into your chocolate). Line molds up on baking sheet. After cocoa butter has melted, dip your artist brush into the brown colored cocoa butter, swipe on inside of each mold cavity, and repeat with pink and yellow colored cocoa butter, cleaning the brush in between colors. Do not clean with water, just wipe clean with a towel. Let sit to dry while melting chocolate. If you prefer not to go through all the extra effort, you can make these without painting the shells.

In a microwave safe bowl, measure out your white compound chocolate. Melt at 30-second increments, stirring in between each addition of time until melted. Pour white compound chocolate into each mold cavity and swirl to coat. Turn mold upside down and shake off excess chocolate. Scrape clean with chocolate scraper. Turn right side up on baking sheet and let dry while you make ganache.

**TO MAKE GANACHE:** In a microwave safe bowl, measure out the white chocolate. Add 200g of heavy cream and melt in microwave at 30-second intervals until melted, stirring in between each addition of time. Split ganache into two bowls.

Add 2ml banana extract and yellow colored cocoa butter to first bowl. Stir well, then pour into piping bag and set aside. To the second bowl, add 2ml strawberry extract and more pink colored cocoa butter (these should still be warm). Pour into piping bag and set aside. In another microwave safe bowl, measure out the second addition of 75g cream to 150g dark chocolate. Melt in microwave at 30-second intervals until melted, stirring in between each addition of time. Add all your cannabis oil to the dark chocolate ganache, stir well to combine, and pour into a piping bag. This part gets a little tricky, but bear with me.

Pipe banana ganache into mold and fill ⅓ of the way. Then pipe strawberry ganache ⅓ of the way, then pipe chocolate ganache into the remaining ⅓ of the mold cavity. Repeat with all mold cavities. Sprinkle with ground pecans and press into chocolate.

**TO FINISH:** Rewarm white compound chocolate, pour over mold, and smooth evenly with an offset spatula. Scrape clean with chocolate scraper. Place molds in fridge for at least 30 minutes to harden. Turn molds over, clean baking sheet, and flex and tap mold to release chocolates. Store in airtight container away from children and pets.

# NEAPOLITAN CHOCOLATES

**The Art of Infusion:**

Go and buy your distillate syringe, wax or shatter, and CBD isolate. Do your recipe calculation using the formula provided. Using your scale, weigh out the amount needed to achieve desired potency. For this recipe, choose whichever ratio you like. The amount needed will be based on the potency of the oil or distillate and isolate you buy. If you bought a gram of shatter that is 88.6 percent, then you will enter 886 into the provided formula. You will need to do the calculation twice. Once for the THC and once for the CBD; if you choose to only use THC, then you will only need to calculate once.

Measure out your cannabis oil and add equal parts MCT oil or coconut oil. Warm in a microwave safe bowl for 15 seconds or in the oven for a few minutes. Measure out CBD isolate and add to hash oil, then add equal parts MCT or coconut oil and warm slightly again. Stir well to combine with a dab tool or fork. Set aside for now.

This is an easy one—no tempering required because that would require three tempering machines. Or you'd have to wait and wash the machine out between each layer, so for the sake of time we are using compound chocolate. You can buy flavor powders at most high-end flavor companies. Just search for flavor powder.

Measure out the white compound chocolate in 2 microwave safe bowls one with 100g and the other with 100g .Microwave at 30-second intervals until melted, stirring in between each addition of time to prevent

INGREDIENTS:
200g white compound chocolate (divided)
100g dark compound chocolate
4 teaspoons vanilla flavor powder
4 teaspoons strawberry flavor powder

TOOLS:
Square chocolate mold
Piping bags
Chocolate scraper
Scale

scorching. Add vanilla flavor powder and ⅓ of your cannabis oil to melted chocolate and mix well. Pour chocolate into piping bag and cut off the tip. Carefully pipe vanilla chocolate into each mold cavity, only ⅓ of the way up. Tap mold to settle chocolate. Melt second addition of white chocolate in microwave at 30 second intervals; add another ⅓ of cannabis oil and strawberry flavor powder. Stir well. Pour chocolate into piping bag and cut off the tip. Pipe another layer of chocolate over the vanilla layer, coming 2/3rds of the way up the mold cavity. Repeat with all mold cavities. Now, measure out dark coating chocolate in microwave at 30-second intervals, stirring in between. Pour in cannabis oil and stir well to combine. Pour chocolate into piping bag and cut off the tip. Pipe the rest of the chocolate over the strawberry layer, coming just to the top of each mold cavity. Tap mold to settle chocolate. Scrape off any excess chocolate and repeat with all the molds.

**TO FINISH:** Place chocolates in fridge to cool for a few minutes (compound chocolate sets quickly). Then turn mold upside down over baking sheet and tap mold to release chocolates.

Store in airtight container away from children and pets.

# CHAPTER SIX

# Baked Goods

You don't see a lot of baked goods in the market, due to their low shelf life; the ones you do see are usually crusty and hard. In my opinion, baked goods should never be hard. Think about it: You go to the gas station and pick up a muffin or pack of donuts; are they hard? No, and who knows how long they've been there? You get my point. I'm not a huge fan of preservatives, but there are some natural preservatives out there that really make a huge difference in baked goods. You eat them all the time; they are in tortillas and bread, among many other things.

As a home chef, you won't have to deal with the challenges of shelf-stability because you will likely eat these up right away. And if they do dry up before you get a chance to eat them, grind them up and mix them into ice cream—yummy! You don't want any of that precious potency to go to waste, right?

It wouldn't be right if we didn't start this section off with a pot brownie. Truth be told, I think my brownies are pretty darn good! Follow my instructions carefully and you will too!

# CLASSIC COOKIE BUTTER SWIRL BROWNIE

**The Art of Infusion:**

Go and buy your distillate syringe, wax or shatter, and CBD isolate. Do your recipe calculation using the formula provided. Using your scale, weigh out the amount needed to achieve desired potency. For this recipe, choose whichever ratio you like. The amount needed will be based on the potency of the oil or distillate and isolate you buy. If you bought a gram of shatter that is 88.6 percent, then you will enter 886 into the provided formula. You will need to do the calculation twice. Once for the THC and once for the CBD; if you choose to only use THC, then you will only need to calculate once.

Measure out your cannabis oil. Add cannabis oil to the fat that's called for in the recipe. That will act as your carrier. In this recipe, the fat will be the butter. Add cannabis oil to butter and melt slowly. Place butter in oven to melt. If using CBD, also add that to the butter and melt in oven. Stir well to combine with a dab tool or fork. Set aside for now.

Measure out your chocolate. Add melted butter/cannabis oil mixture to chocolate and melt over a Bain Marie or double boiler. Don't know what this is? Get a saucepot and fill with a little bit of water. Let the water come to a simmer. Place metal mixing bowl with chocolate and butter/cannabis oil mixture over simmering water. Stir constantly until melted. Set aside to cool for now.

Separately measure out sugar, flour, vanilla, and egg yolks. Pour chocolate butter/cannabis oil mixture into mixing bowl. Using whip

INGREDIENTS:
340g flour
365g dark chocolate
270g sugar
2 teaspoons vanilla
8 egg yolks
224g butter

TOPPING:
2 tablespoons cookie butter
200g dark chocolate
50g white chocolate

TOOLS:
Baking sheet
Offset spatula
KitchenAid mixer
Measuring bowls
Scale
Popsicle stick

Add sugar, mix just to combine. Next, add flour again and mix just to combine—do not overmix or the butter will seep out and the brownie will not be fudgy.

Spray a ¼ baking sheet with pan spray and cut out enough parchment paper to fit inside it. Spray parchment paper again and pour brownie batter onto parchment.

Press down into pan and smooth evenly with offset spatula. Bake at 350 degrees for 6 minutes, then turn and bake another 8 minutes. Remove from oven. Bake times may vary due to altitude—check your brownie after recommended time. Shake the brownie batter; if it still jiggles, add a couple more minutes. What you are looking for on this brownie is for batter to be set but still a tiny bit under cooked. We want a fudgy type brownie, so it's important not to overcook the brownie.

**TOPPING:** My grandma taught me this trick, and I have since taught it to all my employees. While the brownie is still hot, sprinkle the second addition of dark chocolate over the top. Let sit and the residual heat will melt the chocolate as the brownie cools.

attachment, whip on medium speed slowly, add egg yolks and vanilla, and whip to a light and fluffy frosting consistency.

Smooth evenly with offset spatula. Now, in a microwave safe bowl, measure out the white chocolate and cookie butter. Melt at 30-second intervals, stirring in between each addition of time until melted. Pour a few spoonfuls over the dark chocolate and swirl with a popsicle stick to create a marble pattern.

**TO FINISH**: Let brownie cool in fridge for at least a few hours. Once cool, cut into squares. Store in airtight container away from children and pets.

# RASPBERRY DREAMSICLE BAR

**The Art of Infusion:**

Go and buy your distillate syringe, wax or shatter, and CBD isolate. Do your recipe calculation using the formula provided. Using your scale, weigh out the amount needed to achieve desired potency. For this recipe, choose whichever ratio you like. The amount needed will be based on the potency of the oil or distillate and isolate you buy. If you bought a gram of shatter that is 88.6 percent, then you will enter 886 into the provided formula. You will need to do the calculation twice. Once for the THC and once for the CBD; if you choose to only use THC, then you will only need to calculate once.

Measure out your cannabis oil. Add cannabis oil to the fat that's called for in the recipe. That will act as your carrier. In this recipe, the fat will be the vegetable oil. Add hash to vegetable oil and melt slowly; place oils in oven to melt. If using CBD, also add that to the oils and melt in oven. Stir well to combine with a dab tool or fork. Set aside for now.

**WARM COCOA BUTTER COLOR:** Fill a small pitcher with water and place in microwave for 2 minutes. Place pink cocoa butter color in hot water and let sit to melt. Shake periodically to temper. Leave in hot water for now.

Using your scale measure, out the white cake mix and add to mixer. Measure out egg yolks, vanilla, and orange cream extract and add to mixer. Pour in your infused vegetable oil. Mix with paddle attachment on medium speed to combine for about 5 minutes. Remove half of the dough and place into metal mixing bowl; set aside for now. Add a few drops of pink food coloring to the other half of the dough and mix to combine with paddle attachment. Preheat oven to 350 degrees. Spray a ¼ sheet pan with pan spray and cut parchment to fit inside bottom of pan. Spray again with pan spray. Pinch off chunks of the white dough and place randomly around baking sheet. Then, take chunks of pink dough and place randomly around the baking

sheet. Wear gloves and press dough down evenly into pan. Push the colors together and use the offset spatula to smooth the top evenly. Bake in oven at 350 degrees for 8 minutes, then turn and bake another 4 minutes. Remove from oven and sprinkle with 200g white chocolate. Let the residual heat melt the chocolate while you prep the raspberry orange chocolate.

**TO FINISH:** Melt second addition 50g of white chocolate in microwave at 30-second intervals, stirring in between each addition of time. Add a few drops of pink colored cocoa butter and raspberry powder to white chocolate and mix well. Smooth white chocolate evenly across the cake with offset spatula. Then using a spoon, drizzle raspberry chocolate over white chocolate and swirl with a popsicle stick to create a marble pattern. Put cake in fridge to cool for a few hours. Remove cake from fridge and cut into squares. Store in airtight container away from children and pets.

INGREDIENTS:
428g white cake mix
104g eggs
61g vegetable oil
2 teaspoons orange cream
    extract
1 teaspoon vanilla
2 teaspoons raspberry flavor
    powder
Pink food color
Pink colored cocoa butter
200g white chocolate
50g white chocolate

TOOLS:
Offset spatula
KitchenAid mixer
Scale
Measuring spoons
Measuring cup

# PEANUT BUTTER SWIRL BROWNIE

**The Art of Infusion:**

Go and buy your distillate syringe, wax or shatter, and CBD isolate. Do your recipe calculation using the formula provided. Using your scale, weigh out the amount needed to achieve desired potency. For this recipe, choose whichever ratio you like. The amount needed will be based on the potency of the oil or distillate and isolate you buy. If you bought a gram of shatter that is 88.6 percent, then you will enter 886 into the provided formula. You will need to do the calculation twice. Once for the THC and once for the CBD; if you choose to only use THC, then you will only need to calculate once.

Measure out your cannabis oil. Add cannabis oil to the fat that's called for in the recipe. That will act as your carrier. In this recipe, the fat will be the butter. Add cannabis oil to butter and melt slowly in oven. If using CBD, also add that to the butter and melt in oven. Stir well to combine with a dab tool or fork. Set aside for now.

**TO MAKE BROWNIE:** Measure out your chocolate. Add melted butter/cannabis oil mixture to chocolate and melt over a Bain Marie or double boiler. Don't know what this is? Get a saucepot and fill with a little bit of water. Let the water come to a simmer. Place metal mixing bowl with chocolate and butter/cannabis oil mixture over simmering water and stir constantly until melted. Set aside to cool for now.

INGREDIENTS:
340g flour
340g dark chocolate
270g sugar
2 teaspoons vanilla
8 egg yolks
224g butter

TOPPING:
2 tablespoons peanut butter
200g dark chocolate
50g white chocolate

TOOLS:
Baking sheet
Offset spatula
KitchenAid mixer
Measuring bowls
Scale
Popsicle stick

Separately, measure out sugar, flour, vanilla, and egg yolks. Pour chocolate butter/cannabis oil mixture into KitchenAid mixing bowl. Using whip attachment, whip on medium speed. Slowly add egg yolks and vanilla and whip to a light and fluffy frosting consistency. Then add sugar. Mix just to combine, then add flour. Again, mix just to combine; do not overmix.

Spray a ¼ baking sheet with pan spray and cut out enough parchment paper to fit inside it. Spray parchment paper again and pour brownie batter onto parchment.

Smooth evenly with offset spatula. Bake at 350 degrees for 8 minutes, then turn and bake for another 6 minutes. Remove from oven. Bake times may vary due to altitude; start with suggested time and add a couple minutes at a time. Keep a close eye on the brownie as it cooks. We are looking for the brownie batter to be set, meaning it doesn't move when jiggled. We want this brownie slightly under baked, as it creates a nice fudgy texture.

**TOPPING**: My grandma taught me this trick. While the brownie is still hot, sprinkle the second addition of dark chocolate over the top. Let sit, and the residual heat will melt the chocolate as the brownie cools. Smooth evenly with offset spatula. Now in microwave safe bowl, measure out the white chocolate and peanut butter. Melt at 30-second intervals, stirring in between each addition of time until melted. Pour a few spoonfuls over the dark chocolate and swirl with a popsicle stick to create a marble pattern. If you don't want the marble pattern, you can also spread the peanut butter chocolate over the brownie first, then melt the dark chocolate and spread over the top.

**TO FINISH**: Let the brownie cool in fridge for at least an hour. Once cool, cut into squares. Store in airtight container away from children and pets.

# NEVERLAND BROOKIE

I'm a lover of both cookies and brownies, so naturally I'm a huge fan of brookies: a cookie-brownie hybrid! The recipe seems advanced, but it's not like all my other recipes. It just takes a little extra time and effort but trust me, in the end it'll all be worth it. Just work through the recipe slowly and be sure to read everything from start to finish before beginning. The brownie portion of this recipe is the infused part because there are no interferents in the dough, such as pretzels or chocolate chips that can cause inconsistent potency.

**The Art of Infusion:**
Go and buy your distillate syringe, wax or shatter, and CBD isolate. Do your recipe calculation using the formula provided. Using your scale, weigh out the amount needed to achieve desired potency. For this recipe, choose whichever ratio you like. The amount needed will be based on the potency of the oil or distillate and isolate you buy. If you bought a gram of shatter that is 88.6 percent, then you will enter 886 into the provided formula. You will need to do the calculation twice. Once for the THC and once for the CBD; if you choose to only use THC, then you will only need to calculate once.

Measure out your hash oil. Add cannabis oil to the fat that's called for in the recipe. That will act as your carrier. In this recipe, the fat will be the butter. Add cannabis oil to butter and place in over to melt slowly. If using CBD, also add that to the butter and melt in oven. Stir well to combine with a dab tool or fork. Set aside for now.

INGREDIENTS:

For the cookie layer:
1 egg
½ cup Peter Pan Peanut Butter, creamy
1 ¼ cup all-purpose flour
¾ cup brown sugar
¼ cup sugar
½ teaspoon Maldon salt
1 teaspoon vanilla
½ cup butter
¼ cup crushed pretzels
¼  cup chocolate chips
¼ cup chopped peanuts

For the brownie layer
340g flour
340g dark chocolate
270g sugar
1 teaspoon vanilla
8 egg yolks
227g butter

TOOLS:
¼ baking sheet
Offset spatula
Measuring spoons
Mixer
Measuring cups
Scale

**TO MAKE THE COOKIE LAYER:** In bowl of mixer, whip the butter and sugars until light, white, and fluffy. It helps if you soften the butter for 10 seconds in microwave. Scrape down the bottom and sides of the bowl and add your eggs, vanilla, and salt. Whip again until frosting consistency. Scrape down bottom and sides of bowl and add your peanut butter. Whip again to combine. Scrape down bottom and sides of bowl again and add your sifted flour and baking soda. Mix on low speed until dough forms. Add in your crushed pretzels, peanuts, and chocolate chips. Spray your ¼ baking sheet with pan spray and cut out parchment paper to fit the bottom of it.

**PRO TIP:** Tear off a big section of parchment, then place the pan on top and trace around it. When you cut it out and place it in pan, it should fit perfectly.

Press the cookie dough into the pan as evenly as possible. Spread evenly with offset spatula. Bake in oven at 350 degrees for 8 minutes, then turn and bake for another 4 minutes. The cookie looks underbaked, right? That's good, because you are going to bake it again when you put the brownie layer on, so it's important not to overbake the cookie part or the whole thing will end up dry. Set aside in fridge to cool while you make the brownie layer.

**TO MAKE THE BROWNIE LAYER:** Clean mixing bowl and all utensils. Measure out dark chocolate and add melted infused butter to it. Melt over a double boiler on low heat, stirring constantly. Let cool for about 10 minutes, then pour into mixing bowl. Add egg yolks and vanilla and whip with whip attachment until light and fluffy. Add sugar and mix just to combine. Add flour and mix just until flour is adsorbed.

Pour brownie batter over cookie layer and smooth evenly with offset spatula. Put brookie back in oven and bake at 350 degrees for 8 minutes, then turn and bake another 6 minutes. Remove from oven and let cool in fridge overnight before cutting. Cut into squares and store in airtight container away from children and pets.

# MONSTER BROOKIE

Dubbed the monster brookie because yes, the cookie layer is blue! And it's stuffed with three different kinds of cookies. Again, the recipe seems intense but it's super easy; just take your time and read through the recipe to make sure you understand everything before you begin.

**The Art of Infusion:**

Go and buy your distillate syringe, wax or shatter, and CBD isolate. Do your recipe calculation using the formula provided. Using your scale, weigh out the amount needed to achieve desired potency. For this recipe, choose whichever ratio you like. The amount needed will be based on the potency of the oil or distillate and isolate you buy. If you bought a gram of shatter that is 88.6 percent, then you will enter 886 into the provided formula. You will need to do the calculation twice. Once for the THC and once for the CBD; if you choose to only use THC, then you will only need to calculate once.

Measure out your hash oil. Add cannabis oil to the fat that's called for in the recipe. That will act as your carrier. In this recipe, the fat will be the butter. Add cannabis oil to butter and place in over to melt slowly. If using CBD, also add that to the butter and melt in oven. Stir well to combine with a dab tool or fork. Set aside for now.

**TO MAKE THE COOKIE LAYER:** Soften the butter for 10 seconds in the microwave, then add to the mixer bowl. Add brown sugar and white sugar and whip until light and fluffy. Add eggs, vanilla, and salt. Whip again until light and fluffy. Sift together the flour, baking powder, and baking soda (I like to do this over parchment paper, then pick up both ends and use as a funnel). Add to mixing bowl and mix just until adsorbed. Add your crushed cookies and mix again to combine. Spray a ¼ baking sheet and cut parchment paper to fit inside it. Press cookie dough down onto baking sheet as evenly as possible. Smooth evenly with offset spatula. Bake at 350 degrees for 8 minutes, then turn and bake for another 4 minutes. Remove from oven and let cool while you make the brownie layer.

**TO MAKE THE BROWNIE LAYER:** Clean mixing bowl and all utensils. Measure out dark chocolate and add melted infused butter to it. Melt over a double boiler on low heat, stirring constantly. Let cool for about 10 minutes, then pour into mixing bowl. Add eggs and vanilla and whip with whip attachment until light and fluffy. Add sugar and mix just to combine. Add flour and mix just until flour is adsorbed.

Pour brownie batter over cookie layer and smooth evenly with offset spatula. Put brookie back in oven and bake at 350 degrees for 8 minutes, then turn and bake for another 6 minutes. More time may be needed depending on altitude— what you are looking for is for the brownie batter to be set meaning, it doesn't move when jiggled. We want this brownie to be a little underbaked so that the brownie is nice and fudge-like. Remove from oven and let cool in fridge overnight before cutting. Cut into squares and store in airtight container away from children and pets.

INGREDIENTS:

For The Cookie Layer:
3 ⅓ cups of flour
1 ½ teaspoons baking powder
1 ¼ teaspoons baking soda
1 ½ teaspoons salt
2 ½ sticks softened butter
1 ¼ cups brown sugar
1 cup sugar
2 eggs
2 teaspoons vanilla
¼ cup crushed regular Oreos
¼ cup crushed Peanut Butter
    Oreos
¼ cup crushed chocolate chip
    cookies

For The Brownie Layer:
340g flour
340g dark chocolate
270g sugar
1 teaspoon vanilla
8 egg yolks
227g butter

TOOLS:
¼ baking sheet
Offset spatula
Measuring spoons
4 qt Mixer
Measuring cups
Scale

# CHAPTER SEVEN

# Hard Candy

I use isomalt in my hard candies, as it helps repel humidity. This keeps them from getting sticky. Depending on your climate, if you're still having trouble getting the texture quite right , take the temperature up to 300-310 degrees. another one of my secrets to making stunning candies is to use very little food color. This will result in a gorgeous almost stained glass effect. As seen in my sour wild berry candies.

# BLUEBERRY LEMONADE

Batch Weight: 723g | Unit Weight: 6g This could change depending on the mold you use. | Yield: 120

This recipe calls for isomalt, which is a type of sugar alcohol. It has a lower glycemic index, so it's safe for diabetics and is mostly used in sugar-free candy and to make sugar sculptures. I like to use it in a 50/50 ratio in my hard candies because it keeps them from getting sticky. Another thing that will help you with this is making sure that you bring the candy all the way up to 300 degrees. Also, be sure that you have a good candy thermometer. As I mentioned in the tools section, I use a thermapen; they are super accurate. A regular candy thermometer will also work. This is also a little bit more of an advanced recipe, but if you feel you're not ready to tackle it, skip down to the Sour Wild Berry recipe.

**The Art of Infusion:**

Go and buy your distillate syringe, wax or shatter, and CBD isolate. Do your recipe calculation using the formula provided. Using your scale, weigh out the amount needed to achieve desired potency. For this recipe, choose whichever ratio you like. The amount needed will be based on the potency of the oil or distillate and isolate you buy. If you bought a gram of shatter that is 88.6 percent, then you will enter 886 into the provided formula. You will need to do the calculation twice. Once for the THC and once for the CBD; if you choose to only use THC, then you will only need to calculate once.

INGREDIENTS:
224g sugar
224g isomalt
175g 42 DE corn syrup
2ml blueberry flavor
2ml lemonade flavor
Blue food coloring
Yellow food coloring
250g water

TOOLS:
Pastry Brush
Saucepan
Glass measuring pitcher
Silicone candy molds
Wooden Spoon
Scale
Sugar gloves
Thermapen or candy
    thermometer

Measure out your cannabis oil. In this section, you will add cannabis oil directly to the pan with the sugars. I find it easiest to warm the cannabis oil, then weigh it out onto a small piece of parchment paper, then place the parchment paper in fridge to cool. The cannabis oil will harden and remove easily; you can just pick it up off the paper and toss it in the pan. You will throw in the cannabis oil at the very end of the recipe so that you don't lose any potency due to heat degradation.

**TO MAKE CANDY:** Using your scale, measure out water and add it to the pan. Measure out sugar, add to saucepan. Measure out isomalt, add to saucepan. Measure out corn syrup, add to pan. Stir once to combine and wet. Bring the sugars to a boil over medium heat. Cook and boil until sugar reaches 300 degrees.

**NOTE:** It takes a while for the sugar to reach 260, but when it does it will go from 260-300 very quickly. Never leave sugar unattended while cooking.

Fill a pitcher or glass with water and as the sugar crystals form on the sides of the pot, dip your pastry brush into the water and swirl along the sides of the pan to wash down the sugar crystals (be sure not to touch the sugar surface with your brush). Once the sugar reaches 300 degrees, remove from heat and stir until temp drops to 250. Drop in your cannabis oil and stir until the cannabis oil is thoroughly mixed in.

Now for the tricky part—MAKE SURE YOU WEAR SUGAR GLOVES. Pour half of the sugar into a glass measuring pitcher. Stir in the blueberry flavor and blue food coloring. Stir well with a spoon (set the other half aside for now).

**PRO TIP**: If the sugar gets too viscous, you can microwave it for 15 seconds to rewarm it, then stir again and pour.

Put on your sugar gloves and pour blue sugar into molds, filling only half way up. Repeat until all sugar is gone. Again, if the sugar thickens and becomes hard to pour, just rewarm for a few seconds in the microwave. I know, I know, the microwave is my best friend.

Now take the rest of the sugar that's in the pan and rewarm it on the stove, stirring constantly over very low heat until sugar is fluid again. Stir in the yellow food coloring and lemonade flavor. Pour sugar into another glass measuring pitcher and pour into candy molds over the blue layer, filling all the way to the top. Repeat with the rest of the molds until all the sugar is poured. Rewarm if necessary.

**TO FINISH**: Let candies sit for at least 30 minutes to harden. Then pop the candies out of the mold; they should come out easily if you used a silicone mold. Place candies in an airtight container and store away from children and pets.

# SOUR WILDBERRY CANDY

Batch Weight: 723g | Unit Weight: 6g This could change depending on the mold you use. | Yield: 120

You can make this candy sour like a War Head by spraying the outside with liquid citric acid. Be sure not to use too much or the sugar will melt.

**The Art of Infusion:**

Go and buy your distillate syringe, wax or shatter, and CBD isolate. Do your recipe calculation using the formula provided. Using your scale, weigh out the amount needed to achieve desired potency. For this recipe, choose whichever ratio you like. The amount needed will be based on the potency of the oil or distillate and isolate you buy. If you bought a gram of shatter that is 88.6 percent, then you will enter 886 into the provided formula. You will need to do the calculation twice. Once for the THC and once for the CBD; if you choose to only use THC, then you will only need to calculate once.

Measure out your cannabis oil. In this section, you will add cannabis oil directly to the pan with the sugars. I find it easiest to warm the cannabis oil, then weigh it out onto a small piece of parchment paper, then place parchment paper in fridge to cool. The cannabis oil will harden and remove easily; then you can just pick it up off the paper and toss it in the pan.

**TO MAKE CANDY:** Measure out the water and add to saucepan. Measure out sugar, add to saucepan. Measure out corn syrup, add to saucepan. Measure out isomalt, add to saucepan. Cook over medium heat; do not stir periodically. Wash down the sugar crystals with a pastry brush (fill

INGREDIENTS:
224g sugar
224g isomalt
175g 42 DE corn syrup
200g water
2 teaspoons citric acid
1 teaspoon malic acid
6ml wildberry flavor
Maroon food coloring

TOOLS:
Saucepan
Scale
Sugar gloves
Pastry brush
Glass measuring pitcher
Silicone candy molds

a glass with water and dip your pastry brush into it. Swirl the brush on sides of pot to wash down crystals as they form). This keeps the sugar crystals from seeding the sugar and causing crystallization. Once the sugar has reached 300 degrees, remove from heat and let cool to 250 degrees. Drop in your cooled cannabis oil, flavoring, color, and acids. Stir well to combine. Make sure you add color before acid.

Next, put your sugar gloves on and carefully pour sugar into a glass measuring pitcher. Pour sugar into molds and fill to the top. If sugar cools and becomes too viscous to pour, rewarm by placing pitcher in microwave for 15-30 seconds. Stir until bubbles subside and then continue pouring. Repeat until all sugar is poured. ALWAYS, ALWAYS wear sugar gloves.

**TO FINISH:** Let candy sit in molds for at least 30 minutes to cool, then pop candies out of mold; they should come out nicely if you used a silicone mold. Spray candies with liquid citric acid for an extra pucker or coat in a sugar citric acid mix. Store in an airtight container away from children and pets.

# BLACKBERRIES & CREAM HARD CANDY

Batch Weight: 723g | Unit Weight: 6g | Yield: 120g

The titanium dioxide in this recipe is what makes the candy creamy; it also enhances the mouthfeel and makes the white whiter. Available online.

**The Art of Infusion:**
Go and buy your distillate syringe, wax or shatter, and CBD isolate. Do your recipe calculation using the formula provided. Using your scale, weigh out the amount needed to achieve desired potency. For this recipe, choose whichever ratio you like. The amount needed will be based on the potency of the oil or distillate and isolate you buy. If you bought a gram of shatter that is 88.6 percent, then you will enter 886 into the provided formula. You will need to do the calculation twice. Once for the THC and once for the CBD; if you choose to only use THC, then you will only need to calculate once.

Measure out your hash oil. In this section, you will add cannabis oil directly to the pan with the sugars. I find it easiest to warm the cannabis oil and weigh it out onto a small piece of parchment paper, then place parchment paper in fridge to cool. The cannabis oil will harden and remove easily; then you can just pick it up off the paper and toss it in the pan. You will throw in the cannabis oil at the very end of the recipe so that you don't lose any potency due to heat degradation.

**TO MAKE CANDY:** Measure out the water and add to saucepan, then measure out the sugar and add to saucepan. Measure the corn syrup and add to saucepan, then measure out the isomalt and add to saucepan. Cook over medium heat; do not stir periodically. Wash down the sugar crystals with a pastry brush (fill a glass with water and dip your pastry brush into it. Swirl the brush on sides of pot to wash down crystals as they form). This keeps the sugar crystals from seeding the sugar and causing crystallization. Once the sugar has reached 300 degrees, remove from heat and let cool to 250 degrees. Drop in your cannabis oil, flavoring, titanium dioxide, coloring, and malic acid—in that order. Stir well to combine.

Next, put your sugar gloves on and carefully pour sugar into a glass measuring pitcher. Pour sugar into molds and fill to the top. If sugar cools and becomes too viscous to pour, rewarm by placing pitcher in microwave for 15-30 seconds. Stir until bubbles subside and then continue pouring. Repeat until all sugar is poured. If you want to make this a double-layer candy, split the sugar into two glass measuring pitchers. Add blackberry flavor to one and cream and titanium dioxide to the other. Pour the cream layer first, then pour in blackberry layer. You can also mix both colors and flavors together as pictured. The double layer is more effort, but more "wow."

**TO FINISH:** Let candy sit in molds for at least 30 minutes. Then pop candy out of molds; they should release nicely if you used silicone molds. Store in an airtight container away from children and pets.

INGREDIENTS:
224g sugar
224g isomalt
275g 42 DE corn syrup
250g water
⅛th teaspoon titanium dioxide
1 teaspoon malic acid
3ml blackberry flavor
3ml cream soda flavor
Purple food coloring

TOOLS:
Saucepan
Scale
Sugar gloves
Pastry brush
Glass measuring pitcher
Silicone candy molds
Thermapen

# GALAXY CANDY

**Batch Weight: 870g  |  Unit Weight: 4g  |  Yield: 217**

This one is one of my most impressive creations. People always give me shit because I'm constantly putting glitter on everything. Disco Dust is something I discovered early in my pastry career. We used to dust the tops of truffles with it in fine dining; needless to say, I was a huge fan! You can buy this online or at specialty cake shops. One of the things I love most about this creation is that it looks complicated but it's SOOO easy. The black gives a nice backdrop and makes the sparkles pop.

### The Art of Infusion:

Go and buy your distillate syringe, wax or shatter, and CBD isolate. Do your recipe calculation using the formula provided. Using your scale, weigh out the amount needed to achieve desired potency. For this recipe, choose whichever ratio you like. The amount needed will be based on the potency of the oil or distillate and isolate you buy. If you bought a gram of shatter that is 88.6 percent, then you will enter 886 into the provided formula. You will need to do the calculation twice. Once for the THC and once for the CBD; if you choose to only use THC, then you will only need to calculate once.

Measure out your cannabis oil. In this section, you will add cannabis oil directly to the pan with the sugars. I find it easiest to warm the cannabis oil and weigh it out onto a small piece of parchment paper, then place parchment paper in fridge to coo. The cannabis oil will harden and remove easily; then you can just pick it up off the paper and toss it

INGREDIENTS:
224g sugar
224g isomalt
275g 42 DE corn syrup
250g water
4ml grape flavoring
Black food coloring
Disco Dust

TOOLS:
Pastry brush
2 glass measuring pitchers
Saucepan
Silicone candy molds
Thermapen
Sugar gloves
Scale
Small pastry brush

in the pan. You will throw in the cannabis oil at the very end of the recipe so that you don't lose any potency due to heat degradation.

**TO MAKE CANDY**: Measure out the water and add to saucepan, then measure out the sugar and add to saucepan. Measure the corn syrup and add to saucepan, then measure out the isomalt and add to saucepan. Stir once to wet the sugars. Cook without stirring over medium heat until sugar reaches 300 degrees. Periodically, wash down crystals from sides of pot (dip pastry brush in water and swirl around sides of pot to wash down sugar crystals as they form). Once the sugar reaches 300 degrees, remove from heat. Let cool to 250 degrees. Toss in your cannabis oil and stir well to combine. Put sugar gloves on and pour half of the sugar into one glass measuring pitcher; pour the other half into the other measuring pitcher. Add a few drops of black food coloring and the grape flavoring to the first pitcher. Rewarm if necessary in the microwave for 15 seconds. Stir until bubbles subside, then pour into molds, filling halfway up. Once you've poured all the black sugar, take out your small artist brush, dip into Disco Dust, and tap artist brush over the black candy layer.

Next, rewarm your second addition of sugar; you will not add any flavor or color to this pitcher. Pour clear sugar over black layer and fill to the top. Repeat with the rest of the candy. If you do add flavor to this layer, make sure that it's clear.

Voilà! You are done, I told you it was easy. Let candy sit in molds to harden for at least 30 minutes, then pop candies out of molds. Store in airtight container away from children and pets.

# ROOT BEER FIZZ LOLLIPOP

**The Art of Infusion:**

Go and buy your distillate syringe, wax or shatter, and CBD isolate. Do your recipe calculation using the formula provided. Using your scale, weigh out the amount needed to achieve desired potency. For this recipe, choose whichever ratio you like. The amount needed will be based on the potency of the oil or distillate and isolate you buy. If you bought a gram of shatter that is 88.6 percent, then you will enter 886 into the provided formula. You will need to do the calculation twice. Once for the THC and once for the CBD; if you choose to only use THC, then you will only need to calculate once. I find it easiest to pre-measure your cannabis oil before weighing out ingredients onto a piece of parchment paper, then placing in the fridge to cool. The oil will harden, and you can just pick it up and toss it in. CBD you would just pour in as isolate.

**TO MAKE CANDY:** Measure out sugar, water, corn syrup, and isomalt into sauce

**INGREDIENTS:**
557g sugar
557g isomalt
354g 42 DE corn syrup
¼ teaspoon malic acid
2 teaspoons root beer flavor
Ground Texturas Fizzy
894g water

**TOOLS:**
Saucepot
Wooden spoon
Glass measuring pitcher
Measuring spoons
Scale
Thermometer
Sugar gloves
Pastry brush

pot. Bring to a boil over medium high heat. Periodically wash down sugar crystals as they form from sides of pot using water and a pastry brush. Cook until sugar reaches 300 degrees on your thermometer. Remove from heat and let cool to 250; toss in your cannabis oil and stir well. Then add color if desired, flavor, and finally acid. If you are wondering why there's acid in this recipe, don't worry. It's there for flavor enhancement, not to add sourness. Stir well, then pour into a glass measuring pitcher. WEAR SUGAR GLOVES and pour candy into lollipop molds. If sugar becomes too viscous, rewarm by placing measuring pitcher in microwave for a few seconds, stir, and continue to pour. Repeat with all molds and all candy. While candy is still warm, dust with ground fizzy powder. I also added a little extra root beer flavor to my fizzy powder.

# ORANGE CREAM FIZZ LOLLIPOP

**The Art of Infusion:**

Go and buy your distillate syringe, wax or shatter, and CBD isolate. Do your recipe calculation using the formula provided. Using your scale, weigh out the amount needed to achieve desired potency. For this recipe, choose whichever ratio you like. The amount needed will be based on the potency of the oil or distillate and isolate you buy. If you bought a gram of shatter that is 88.6 percent, then you will enter 886 into the provided formula. You will need to do the calculation twice. Once for the THC and once for the CBD; if you choose to only use THC, then you will only need to calculate once. I find it easiest to pre-measure your cannabis oil before weighing out ingredients onto a piece of parchment paper, then placing in the fridge to cool. The oil will harden, and you can just pick it up and toss it in. CBD you would just pour in as isolate.

INGREDIENTS:
557g sugar
557g isomalt
354g corn syrup
894g water
½ teaspoon malic acid
2 teaspoons orange cream
    flavor
Ground Texturas Fizzy
Orange food coloring

TOOLS:
Saucepot
Wooden spoon
Glass measuring pitcher
Measuring spoons
Scale
Thermometer
Sugar gloves
Pastry brush

**TO MAKE CANDY**: Measure out sugar, water, corn syrup, and isomalt into sauce pot. Bring to a boil over medium high heat. Periodically wash down sugar crystals as they form from sides of pot using water and a pastry brush. Cook until sugar reaches 300 degrees on your thermometer. Remove from heat and let cool to 250; toss in your cannabis oil and stir well. Then add color if desired, flavor, and finally acid. Stir well, then pour into a glass measuring pitcher. WEAR SUGAR GLOVES and pour candy into lollipop molds. If sugar becomes too viscous, rewarm by placing measuring pitcher in microwave for a few seconds. Stir and continue to pour. Repeat with all molds and all candy. While candy is still warm, dust with ground fizzy powder. I added cream soda flavor to my fizzy powder; this is optional.

# STRAWBERRY WATERMELON COCONUT LOLLIPOP

Sounds weird, but I promise it's delicious!

**The Art of Infusion:**

Go and buy your distillate syringe, wax or shatter, and CBD isolate. Do your recipe calculation using the formula provided. Using your scale, weigh out the amount needed to achieve desired potency. For this recipe, choose whichever ratio you like. The amount needed will be based on the potency of the oil or distillate and isolate you buy. If you bought a gram of shatter that is 88.6 percent, then you will enter 886 into the provided formula. You will need to do the calculation twice. Once for the THC and once for the CBD; if you choose to only use THC, then you will only need to calculate once. I find it easiest to pre-measure your cannabis oil before weighing out ingredients onto a piece of parchment paper, then placing in the fridge to cool. The oil will harden, and you can just pick it up and toss it in. CBD you would just pour in as isolate.

**TO MAKE CANDY:** Measure out sugar, water, corn syrup, and isomalt into sauce pot. Bring to a boil over medium high heat. Periodically wash down sugar crystals as they form from sides of pot using water and a pastry brush. Cook until sugar reaches 300 degrees on your thermometer. Remove from heat and let cool to 250; toss in your cannabis oil and stir well. Then add color if desired, flavor, and finally acid. Stir well, then pour into a glass measuring pitcher. WEAR SUGAR GLOVES and pour candy into lollipop molds. If sugar becomes too viscous, rewarm by placing measuring pitcher in microwave for a few seconds. Stir and continue to pour. Repeat with all molds and all candy. I did not add any fizz or sour to this recipe.

INGREDIENTS:
557g sugar
557g isomalt
354g corn syrup
894g water
½ teaspoon malic acid
2ml strawberry flavor
2ml watermelon flavor
1ml coconut flavor
Red food coloring
Pink food coloring

TOOLS:
Saucepot
Wooden spoon
Glass measuring pitcher
Measuring spoons
Scale
Thermometer
Sugar gloves
Pastry brush

# SOUR CRANBERRY LOLLIPOP

**The Art of Infusion:**

Go and buy your distillate syringe, wax or shatter, and CBD isolate. Do your recipe calculation using the formula provided. Using your scale, weigh out the amount needed to achieve desired potency. For this recipe, choose whichever ratio you like. The amount needed will be based on the potency of the oil or distillate and isolate you buy. If you bought a gram of shatter that is 88.6 percent, then you will enter 886 into the provided formula. You will need to do the calculation twice. Once for the THC and once for the CBD; if you choose to only use THC, then you will only need to calculate once. I find it easiest to pre-measure your cannabis oil before weighing out ingredients onto a piece of parchment paper, then placing in the fridge to cool. The oil will harden, and you can just pick it up and toss it in. CBD you would just pour in as isolate.

**TO MAKE CANDY:** Measure out sugar, water, corn syrup, and isomalt into sauce pot. Bring to a boil over medium high heat. Periodically wash down sugar crystals as they form from sides of pot using water and a pastry brush. Cook until sugar reaches 300 degrees on your thermometer. Remove from heat and let cool to 250; toss in your cannabis oil and stir well. Then add color if desired, flavor, and finally acid. Stir well, then pour into a glass measuring pitcher. WEAR SUGAR GLOVES and pour candy into lollipop molds. If sugar becomes too viscous, rewarm by placing measuring pitcher in microwave for a few seconds. Stir and continue to pour. Repeat with all molds and all candy. While candy is still warm, dust with sour sugar citric acid mix.

INGREDIENTS:
557g sugar
557g isomalt
354g corn syrup
894g water
½ teaspoon malic acid
6ml cranberry flavor
Ground sugar citric acid mix
Maroon food coloring

TOOLS:
Saucepot
Wooden spoon
Glass measuring pitcher
Measuring spoons
Scale
Thermometer
Sugar gloves
Pastry brush

CHAPTER EIGHT

# Caramels

Most pastry chefs use the pour and cut method for caramels, but when working with cannabis you need much more consistency. Plus, they look great molded! My grandma taught me how to make this recipe. It's pretty much the same recipe found throughout the book, I just changed the flavoring.

Make sure that you buy a good candy thermometer! One degree over or under in this recipe can make a huge difference. You can buy the Texturas Fizzy in the Citrus Fizz Caramel online, at AUI Fine Foods, or any molecular gastronomy store.

# GERMAN CHOCOLATE CARAMEL

Batch Weight: 447g  |  Unit Weight: 4.7g  |  Yield: 96

German chocolate is not actually German at all; it gets its name from a man who created a dark chocolate bark in 1852 and used it to make the classic cake. His name was Samuel German; this is another example of taking something classic and turning it into something new.

**The Art of Infusion:**

Go and buy your distillate syringe, wax or shatter, and CBD isolate. Do your recipe calculation using the formula provided. Using your scale, weigh out the amount needed to achieve desired potency. For this recipe, choose whichever ratio you like. The amount needed will be based on the potency of the oil or distillate and isolate you buy. If you bought a gram of shatter that is 88.6 percent, then you will enter 886 into the provided formula. You will need to do the calculation twice. Once for the THC and once for the CBD; if you choose to only use THC, then you will only need to calculate once.

Measure out your cannabis oil. In this section, you will add cannabis oil directly to the pan with the sugars. I find it easiest to warm the cannabis oil and weigh it out onto a small piece of parchment paper, then place parchment paper in fridge to cool. The cannabis oil will harden and remove easily; then you can just pick it up off the paper and toss it in the pan. You will throw in the cannabis oil at the very end of the recipe so that you don't lose any potency due to heat degradation.

INGREDIENTS:
83g butter
185g corn syrup
130g brown sugar
113g cream
7g Maldon salt
15g vanilla
40g dark chocolate
40g ground coconut
35g pecan pieces

TOOLS:
Saucepan
Whisk
Piping bags
Scale
Caramel molds
Sugar gloves
Thermapen
Clear candy wrappers

**TO MAKE CARAMELS**: Measure out butter and add to saucepan, measure out corn syrup and add to sauce pan, measure out cream, salt, vanilla, and add to saucepan. Measure out chocolate and coconut set aside for now.

Bring the sugar, cream, corn syrup mixture to a boil over medium heat. Stir constantly with a whisk. Cook and stir until temperature reaches 250 degrees. Remove from heat and stir in cannabis oil, chocolate, and coconut. Whisk well to combine. Let caramel cool slightly, then put sugar gloves on and pour caramel into a piping bag. Pipe caramel into molds and repeat with all caramel and all molds.

Let sit to harden for at least a few hours. Then carefully unmold the caramels and wrap them in candy cellophane (you can buy this online). Store in an airtight container away from children and pets.

# CITRUS FIZZ CARAMEL

Batch Weight: 447g | Unit Weight: 4.7g | Yield: 96

**The Art of Infusion:**

Go and buy your distillate syringe, wax or shatter, and CBD isolate. Do your recipe calculation using the formula provided. Using your scale, weigh out the amount needed to achieve desired potency. For this recipe, choose whichever ratio you like. The amount needed will be based on the potency of the oil or distillate and isolate you buy. If you bought a gram of shatter that is 88.6 percent, then you will enter 886 into the provided formula. You will need to do the calculation twice. Once for the THC and once for the CBD; if you choose to only use THC, then you will only need to calculate once.

Measure out your cannabis oil. In this section, you will add cannabis oil directly to the pan with the sugars. I find it easiest to warm the cannabis oil and weigh it out onto a small piece of parchment paper, then place parchment paper in fridge to cool. The cannabis oil will harden and remove easily; then you can just pick it up off the paper and toss it in the pan. You will throw in the cannabis oil at the very end of the recipe so that you don't lose any potency due to heat degradation.

**TO MAKE CARAMELS**: Measure out butter and add to saucepan, measure out corn syrup and add to sauce pan, measure out cream, salt, vanilla, and lemon juice, and add to saucepan.

INGREDIENTS:
83g butter
185g corn syrup
125g brown sugar
113g cream
7g salt
15g vanilla
4ml citrus blend flavor
Ground Texturas Fizzy

TOOLS:
Saucepan
Whisk
Piping bags
Scale
Caramel molds
Sugar gloves
Thermapen
Clear candy wrappers

Bring the sugar, cream, corn syrup mixture to a boil over medium heat. Stir constantly with a whisk. Cook and stir until temperature reaches 250 degrees. Remove from heat and stir in cannabis oil and citrus blend flavor. Whisk well to combine. Let caramel cool slightly, then put sugar gloves on and pour caramel into a piping bag. Pipe caramel into molds and repeat with all caramel and all molds.

Let sit to harden for at least a few hours. Then carefully unmold the caramels and place them into a bowl. Spray them with pan spray and toss around in the bowl to coat. Then grind up your Texturas Fizzy and sprinkle over caramels, toss to coat, and wrap them in candy cellophane (you can buy this online). Store in an airtight container away from children and pets.

# CRÈME BRULEE CARAMEL

Batch Weight: 447g  |  Unit Weight: 4.7g  |  Yield: 96

Crème brulee is a classical French dessert. It is traditionally a cooked and cooled custard similar to flan but with a caramelized sugar instead of caramel sauce. I have given it a twist and turned it into a caramel. You can still brulee the sugar with a torch but be careful; you might melt it. The raw sugar gives it a nice crunch and the white chocolate softens the caramel so that it doesn't stick to your teeth.

**The Art of Infusion:**

Go and buy your distillate syringe, wax or shatter, and CBD isolate. Do your recipe calculation using the formula provided. Using your scale, weigh out the amount needed to achieve desired potency. For this recipe, choose whichever ratio you like. The amount needed will be based on the potency of the oil or distillate and isolate you buy. If you bought a gram of shatter that is 88.6 percent, then you will enter 886 into the provided formula. You will need to do the calculation twice. Once for the THC and once for the CBD; if you choose to only use THC, then you will only need to calculate once.

Measure out your hash oil. In this section, you will add hash oil directly to the pan with the sugars. I find it easiest to warm the cannabis oil and weigh it out onto a small piece of parchment paper, then place parchment paper in fridge to cool. The cannabis oil will harden and remove easily; then you can just pick it up off the paper and toss it in the pan. You will throw in the cannabis oil at the very end of the recipe so that you don't lose any potency due to heat degradation.

**TO MAKE CARAMELS**: Measure out butter and add to saucepan, measure out corn syrup and add to sauce pan, measure out cream, salt, vanilla, and lemon juice, and add to saucepan. Measure out white chocolate and set aside for now.

Bring the sugar, cream, corn syrup mixture to a boil over medium heat. Stir constantly with a whisk. Cook and stir until temperature reaches 250 degrees. Remove from heat and stir in cannabis oil and white chocolate. Whisk well to combine. Let caramel cool slightly, then put sugar gloves on and pour caramel into a piping bag. Sprinkle raw sugar into each mold cavity, then pipe caramel molds. Repeat with all caramel and all molds. Sprinkle more raw sugar on the tops.

Let sit to harden for at least a few hours, then wrap in candy cellophane (you can buy this online). Store in an airtight container away from children and pets.

INGREDIENTS:
83g butter
185g corn syrup
125g brown sugar
113g cream
7g salt
15g vanilla
40g white chocolate
7g lemon juice
Raw sugar

TOOLS:
Saucepan
Whisk
Piping bags
Scale
Caramel molds
Sugar gloves
Thermapen
Clear candy wrappers

# CIDER CARAMEL

Batch Weight: 447g | Unit Weight: 4.7g | Yield: 96

**The Art of Infusion:**

Go and buy your distillate syringe, wax or shatter, and CBD isolate. Do your recipe calculation using the formula provided. Using your scale, weigh out the amount needed to achieve desired potency. For this recipe, choose whichever ratio you like. The amount needed will be based on the potency of the oil or distillate and isolate you buy. If you bought a gram of shatter that is 88.6 percent, then you will enter 886 into the provided formula. You will need to do the calculation twice. Once for the THC and once for the CBD; if you choose to only use THC, then you will only need to calculate once.

Measure out your cannabis oil. In this section, you will add cannabis oil directly to the pan with the sugars. I find it easiest to warm the cannabis oil and weigh it out onto a small piece of parchment paper, then place parchment paper in fridge to cool. The cannabis oil will harden and remove easily; then you can just pick it up off the paper and toss it in the pan. You will throw in the cannabis oil at the very end of the recipe so that you don't lose any potency due to heat degradation.

**TO MAKE CARAMELS**: Measure out butter and add to saucepan, measure out corn syrup and add to sauce pan, measure out cream, salt, vanilla, and lemon juice, and add to saucepan. Measure out white chocolate and set aside for now.

Bring the sugar, cream, corn syrup mixture to a boil over medium heat. Stir constantly with a whisk. Cook and stir until temperature reaches 245 degrees. Remove from heat and stir in cannabis oil, cider powder, and white chocolate. Whisk well to combine. Let caramel cool slightly, then put sugar gloves on and pour caramel into a piping bag. Sprinkle raw sugar into each mold cavity, then pipe caramel molds. Repeat with all caramel and all molds.

Let sit to harden for at least a few hours, then wrap in candy cellophane (you can buy this online). Store in an airtight container away from children and pets.

INGREDIENTS:
83g butter
185g corn syrup
125g brown sugar
113g cream
7g salt
15g vanilla
40g white chocolate
7g lemon juice
1 packet apple cider powder

TOOLS:
Saucepan
Whisk
Piping bags
Scale
Caramel molds
Sugar gloves
Thermapen
Clear candy wrappers

# RASPBERRY CARAMEL

Batch Weight: 447g I Unit Weight: 4.7g I Yield: 96

**The Art of Infusion:**

Go and buy your distillate syringe, wax or shatter, and CBD isolate. Do your recipe calculation using the formula provided. Using your scale, weigh out the amount needed to achieve desired potency. For this recipe, choose whichever ratio you like. The amount needed will be based on the potency of the oil or distillate and isolate you buy. If you bought a gram of shatter that is 88.6 percent, then you will enter 886 into the provided formula. You will need to do the calculation twice. Once for the THC and once for the CBD; if you choose to only use THC, then you will only need to calculate once.

Measure out your cannabis oil. In this section, you will add cannabis oil directly to the pan with the sugars. I find it easiest to warm the cannabis oil and weigh it out onto a small piece of parchment paper, then place parchment paper in fridge to cool. The cannabis oil will harden and remove easily; then you can just pick it up off the paper and toss it in the pan. You will throw in the cannabis oil at the very end of the recipe so that you don't lose any potency due to heat degradation.

**TO MAKE CARAMELS:** Measure out butter and add to saucepan, measure out corn syrup and add to sauce pan, measure out cream, salt, vanilla, and lemon juice, and add to saucepan. Measure out white chocolate and set aside for now.

Bring the sugar, cream, corn syrup mixture to a boil over medium heat. Stir constantly with a whisk. Cook and stir until temperature reaches 245 degrees. Remove from heat and stir in cannabis oil, and white chocolate. Whisk well to combine. Let caramel cool slightly, then put sugar gloves on and pour caramel into a piping bag. Pipe caramel into molds let set for 24 hours then unmold caramels and dip into ground raspberry powder.

INGREDIENTS:
83g butter
185g corn syrup
125g brown sugar
113g cream
7g salt
15g vanilla
40g white chocolate
7g lemon juice
Ground freeze dried
    raspberries

TOOLS:
Saucepan
Whisk
Piping bags
Scale
Caramel molds
Sugar gloves
Thermapen
Clear candy wrappers

# Acknowledgments

Thank you to my loving husband for always supporting my dreams and goals, and for patiently allowing me to ignore him for months while I wrote this book and made all the recipes. I love you so much.

I want to thank God for blessing me with creative ability and talent.

May I always use my gifts humbly and teach them to others.

Big huge thank you to Kate at Mascot Books for loving this idea and being there to help me make this dream a reality every step of the way! And to my editors Kiley and Nina, you've been amazing!

And thank you of course to you, the reader! I hope you enjoyed reading this book and learned lots of fun new and exciting ways to get creative with cannabis.

Thank you to Layle for supporting me all these years and for writing the foreword.

And lastly, to my tattoo artist and mentor Eddie of Dreambent Studios. "Get your dreams to pay your fucking bills."

# About the Author

Krystina is an award-winning cannabis chef, food scientist, and confectionery consultant. Krystina has developed products, designed kitchens, and implemented process improvements and scaleups for multiple cannabis companies across the US and Canada. She also owns Kaylx Consulting, a cannabis consulting business. She lives in Denver, Colorado with her husband, son, and daughter. Find Krystina Marie on Facebook and follow @_krys_tina_ on Instagram to keep up with her baking adventures.